ONLY THREE-PENCE A BRICK

My Journey During WWII

Don Warner

(Edited by Lynette Sloane)

HÁLORA PRESS

ONLY THREE-PENCE A BRICK
My Journey During WWII

ISBN 978-0-9573610-4-1

First Published 2019 by
Hálora Press

Printed and bound in Great Britain by
Print Resources, Welwyn Garden City, Hertfordshire AL8 7BG.

ONLY THREE-PENCE A BRICK

My Journey During WWII

'Tigre' the only toy I owned as a child.

Hanna Reich, a cook at one of my foster homes, made it out of the lining of an overcoat. Over 75 years later, it is still a reminder of her love for me... the little evacuee lad from London.

Special Thanks

Lynette Sloane (The Author): Thank you for unravelling my scribbles and turning my story into a book. Lynette now refers to me as 'Scribbles', and I refer to her as 'The Writer'.

Ian Grimshaw (Designer): Thank you for designing the front cover and including the photo of myself taken in Bolton when I was 7 ½ years old.

Matthew Taylor: Thank you for typing up my scribbles and urging me to write more. This process took nearly two years.

Doreen Corns (My Sister-in-law): Doreen suggested the title of the book, after listening to my war stories at my home in Spain. (I thought she was asleep.) Thank you.

My wife, Sandy: Sandy made it possible for me to scribble away all night, supplying me with tea and toast at all hours. Thank you for your support.

- Don Warner (Scribbler)

Contents

Preface

The Evacuation of Children During the Second World War.

In the years leading up to the Second World War, fear of the effects of bombing of cities from the air was both deep and widespread, even verging on panic in many European countries— partly based on reports of the destruction of Guernica and other towns during the Spanish Civil War of 1936-39 and of discriminate bombing of civilians by the Japanese Air Force in their attacks China from 1937.

The British authorities anticipated that up to 30,000 civilians would be killed and over 10,000 wounded in the first week of hostilities alone. In reality, these fears were greatly exaggerated. Only later in the war, from 1943 onward, would bomb casualties in Germany and Japan reach anything like the numbers feared, and casualties in Britain, which faced much less intensive bombing than Germany (mainly during 1940-41) amounted to a tiny proportion of the population: some 65,000 fatalities in all. However, given the belief prevalent at the time it made sense for governments to remove non-essential civilians, children in particular, from unnecessary danger by transporting them from cities and large industrial towns to the relative safety of rural areas.

In Britain, planning began as the war-clouds gathered in 1938, with the Ministry of Health coordinating the activities of local authorities. By the declaration of war on Germany on 3rd September 1939, plans were well advanced, and some 300,000 children had left London and other cities on the south and east coasts in special trains—within one week. After the fall of France

7

and the Dunkirk evacuation in June 1940, movements were intensified, and, after the London Blitz began in September, these speeded up still further. As attacks by the Luftwaffe spread country-wide late in 1940 and in the first half of 1941 the evacuation programme was extended to the Midlands and the North, and by late 1941 over 60% of Manchester and Liverpool's child populations over five years old had been evacuated, in the former case mainly to Cheshire and Derbyshire, in the latter case to North Wales, Cheshire, and rural East Lancashire.

Altogether, some 1.4 million British children were evacuated under the official scheme and another unknown number, probably 300,000, at least, by private arrangements between parents and host families, many involving children being sent to relatives living in less threatened areas.

Similar evacuation programmes were undertaken from cities in Northern and Eastern France considered vulnerable to Luftwaffe attack in 1939, and in North and West Germany from late 1941 as night-bombing of German cities by the RAF intensified children were evacuated to safer areas within the Reich or occupied territories, mainly to Bavaria, Austria, Bohemia, or Western Poland. The French programme ended when the June 1940 surrender removed the risk of Luftwaffe bombing and the children had all been returned home by the end of the year; ironically, a second wave of child evacuations began in late 1943 as civilian casualties mounted from Allied Air Forces' attacks on French cities in preparation of the Normandy landings of June 1944. The German programme which was run by the Nazi Party, the Hitler Youth, and the SS, mainly involved moving the children to special camps in the countryside; as one might expect the general ethos was much more militaristic than in the British and French arrangements, but many evacuees' memories, as well as the usual homesickness, include carefree and happy times in a world that was otherwise falling apart, with father and brothers lost on the fearsome battlefronts of the East. Although precise figures are unavailable due to destruction of records in the last months of the war, some 3 million German children were evacuated under one scheme or another and the programme is generally credited with saving the lives of hundreds of thousands from the massive RAF and USAAF bombing of cities during 1943-45 and the heavy ground fighting as German was overrun by Western and Soviet armies in early 1945.

The experience of evacuees in Britain was extraordinarily varied. In some regions most city children were moved, in others very few. The majority of children spend the war in rural homes, but others resided in special camps for boys or girls not unlike those for German children. Many evacuees spend the entire war in the same household; others, as in Don's case, were moved from one residence and one district to another, often with little or no notice and for no reason that made any sense to the child. Most hosts treated the children with love and care but in other homes evacuees were regarded as unpaid domestic or farm labourers; host families received extra rations and payment, but it was not uncommon for the unfortunate children to receive very little of these. In some districts the children were encouraged, even required, to keep in touch with home by frequent letter writing, but in others such contact was disapproved of or even forbidden on the grounds that hearing from home would increase homesickness and make it more difficult for the children to settle into their new surroundings. Stories of homesickness abound in the memories of evacuees; in many cases these were children from poverty stricken urban backgrounds pitched into totally unfamiliar and, at first, challenging rural surroundings.

Looking back at these events from the perspective of seventy-odd years later it's striking how little attention was given to the risks of various kind of abuse of evacuees. Don's account of children being lined up, inspected, selected and then taken away by prospective reception families seems very strange in our eyes.

As the threat of the Luftwaffe dwindled, and from 1942 onwards an increasing number of evacuated children were reclaimed by their parents, despite official disapproval. Some particularly unhappy or enterprising children made their own way home, but the evacuation programme was largely maintained unto the end of the war in Europe in May 1945, and children only began to return to the London area from June 1945 onwards. Don appears to have spent the entire duration of hostilities in a range of foster homes across several regions of the country before being returned to London by parents with whom he'd had no contact for nearly six years. For many evacuees, however, the destruction or damage to over half a million urban homes due to bombing, or the death of parents in the raids or on the battlefield, meant there were no homes for families to return to and a proportion of evacuated children remained in State or foster care for years.

Opinion remains divided as to the success of the evacuation programme. It undoubtedly saved the lives of many children, but probably far fewer in Britain than pre-war planners would have expected, and the effects of prolonged separation from family care, particularly on younger children, have been cited as one of the contributing causes of social alienation, crime, and mental health problems in later decades. As always, with such exercises in social engineering, some evacuees thrived, learned to adapt to changing circumstances and, as in Don's case, went on to make a success of their lives. Others were not so fortunate.

Dr Barry McCarthy

Prologue

What a lucky lad I had been to live through those early happenings. They set me up for life.

I dedicate my thoughts and experiences to anybody who wishes to read them. If you learn anything from them, then this book has been worth the writing. There is always sunshine behind a cloud; you just have to be patient, because the sun will always find you, and that's when your life begins...

Part One

Chapter 1

The Beginning of my Journey

A wet, overcast day in 1939 marked the beginning of the long journey that was to shape my whole life.

I gazed at the pathway and watched the rain drip off my hair into a small puddle.

My mother bent down. Her voice was gentle, and I had to listen carefully to hear what she was saying. "Don, you're going to the countryside to see the ducks."

Everyone around me was much taller than my three year, nine-month-old self. I stared at their wet coats and luggage. It would seem that they were also on their way to see the ducks.

My sister, a little girl four years older than me, was being instructed to hold my hand and never to let go. I gripped the end of the white pillowcase that held my few clothes and possessions and slung it over my shoulder to carry it, confused, as various ladies kissed me repeatedly. Some of them seemed upset about me going to see the ducks. I looked up at my mum and aunt. Both were crying.

My sister held my hand, and we set off on what seemed to be a long walk. The group of ladies waved to us, their eyes brimming with tears.

We eventually arrived outside a school, where hundreds of children had also gathered to see the ducks. A lady took me away from my sister. She tied a large brown ticket to my coat and placed a brown box around my neck. This was my gas mask. Another lady smiled at me and took me off to the toilet.

I can't remember what happened next. All that remains etched on my memory is the feeling I had of being on my own. My sister had been taken to the girls' section, and I was placed with the other infants, many of whom were crying. I wasn't lonely or scared and didn't miss my mum; I was too excited about seeing those ducks. Children ran up and down the large room. I don't think they really wanted to see the ducks. Maybe they just wanted to be naughty.

My next memory is of marching along the road with hundreds of children all holding hands and singing. I was excited and could think of nothing except those ducks.

I'd already forgotten my sister who was supposed to hold my hand, and I didn't see her again for many years.

My next memory, after a long journey on a charabanc coach, was of a lady with a big blue hat. She wore a grey coat with red letters embroidered onto a sewn-on badge. I found out many years later she was a member of the Women's Voluntary Service (later known as 'the army Hitler forgot').

She took me with other children to a house in Bracklesham Bay, West Sussex, where we were to stay, and led us along a path and into a garden where there was a large greenhouse. We stepped inside. I took a deep breath and stared up at the bunks which were stacked three high. I'd never seen so many beds. Because I was one of the smaller ones, they allocated me a bottom bunk.

We removed the cardboard boxes from around our necks, took off our shoes, and were instructed to rest. This directive didn't prove very successful as some children were crying and one or two wet themselves, but I managed to get some sleep.

Sometime later I remember being taken into a hall where many children ran around playing and others were crying. We were all given a slice of bread and dripping and a warm cup of cocoa. When we had finished, we were told to play in the grounds of the house. This was very exciting to a small lad.

We ran into the garden and began exploring. At the bottom of the grounds, past the trees and flowerbeds, we discovered a large wall with water splashing over the top. The older children climbed up to look over the wall and I wanted to do the same, but I was too little. However, an older boy lifted me up. My mouth dropped open at the site before me. I'd never seen the sea. It seemed to go on forever. The waves rushed in towards me and hit the rocks and the spray flew up and splashed over the wall. I stared, wide-eyed and was a little disappointed when the older boy, who seemed to be looking after me, put me down on the lawn. Still exhilarated, we continued running about the garden, having great fun.

The next day, the ladies took us on an outing to the seaside. We picked wild flowers along the wayside then poured onto the stony beach. Ahead of me, wooden steps led up to a pier reaching out into the sea where fishermen tied their fishing boats whilst unloading their catch.

The older children and a lady from the WVS ran across the beach, up the steps, and along the platform. Another lady helper realised the steps were too big for my little legs so took my hand and helped me climb them. I reached the top step and gazed down at the sea below listening to the waves pushing up the beach and dragging the rounded pebbles back into the sea.

I took a few tentative steps along the decking. The gaps between the planks were larger than my tiny feet and I could see the swirling water below. The helpers hadn't taken this into account. I took another step and felt myself falling. I cried out. My right foot had gone down through a gap and my leg was stuck fast with the cold water lapping around it. My other leg was trapped under my body. Tears ran down my face as I watched my shoe floating around in the sea.

14

The two ladies grabbed hold of me and tried to free my leg, but it was stuck fast. A man did something with the wood which formed the decking and eventually freed me. He carried me to a waiting car and drove me to the cottage hospital.

I sat on the hospital bed and stared down at my leg. A deep cut ran from my ankle to my knee, and my kneecap rested to one side where it had been displaced. I remember blood and pain and ladies rushing around. Having left Tooting only four days before, I was now in hospital... and had not yet sighted a single duck. To this day when my knee is under stress, it gives way and aches for days.

The ladies in blue cared for me until my leg healed. One of them took me home with her and I remember her little dog jumping all over me. I still have a photo of that dog.

Upon my release from the cottage hospital, I was taken to a large country house near Selsey Bill in Sussex. I'd been very lucky to have had the accident. Some years later I discovered the home I stayed in at Bracklesham Bay was hit by several bombs when a German bomber offloaded on his way back to his base. Many people were killed including some of the children I'd played with.

Chapter 2

Moving On

I don't recall how long I stayed at Selsey Bill, but I remember sleeping in a wooden shed with bunk beds; again, on a bottom bunk.

Several girls and boys stayed at the estate. At meal times, the adults kept the little ones to one side, but afterwards we all mixed together.

Soon I was diagnosed with impetigo, contracted either from the straw, or from other children, and was taken back to the hospital where a doctor examined me. He confirmed the earlier diagnosis, and, as antibiotics were only just being developed and were not widely available, I was stripped naked and placed in what seemed to be a glass box with a group of children who were all bigger than me. The girls were naked as well and I was amazed that they were different to me. We shut our eyes tight as we were sprayed with a yellow powder known as crystal violet. It made us all smell funny. Afterwards, a nurse gave us something to eat on a teaspoon.

Next, she painted our fingers, legs and feet with a blue dye. This process was repeated twice a week. I looked down at myself. I was multi-coloured and still had a bad knee—what fun I was having in the countryside. At least I'd seen lots of ducks and seeing them now became an everyday event.

My fellow evacuees and I shared the same predicament; we didn't understand why we were away from home but tried to make the best of it. Some boys acted tough during the day, but, alone in their bunks at night, hidden in the darkness, their insecurities bubbled over and they screamed and cried. I never cried or got really upset. The many things I'd experienced since leaving London gave me much to think about, and eventually, even the ducks were forgotten.

Because I was so young it has been difficult to remember all the moves I went through, and some have completely gone from my memory, erased by the passing of time. I find it remarkable that when I look at a map, or someone mentions a place or name in conversation, I get a shock or vision and know I once lived there. Immediately, my mind works overtime. It's frustrating to hear a place name and know that at some stage of your young life you have lived there but can't remember any details.

One such place was Chesil Bank in Dorset. My memory tells me I lived there for a short while in a large house with two other children both older than me. I was so small I needed help to climb up the front steps. A girl would take my hand and help me while she carried her little dog under her other arm.

I also recall being in a car which had an unfamiliar smell. I learned in later life that this was leather. To this day whenever I smell leather my mind goes back to that car ride even though I have no idea where it was or when it took place.

Memories of this time come back to me and ebb away much like the tide. I remember looking at a group of men standing on the beach. Some wore military uniform and held long pieces of wood. Others carried guns over their shoulders. There was shouting and loud bangs, which I later learned was artillery fire. The whole area was very noisy, and soldiers marched up and down. We weren't allowed to set foot on that beach. I didn't understand what was happening; it was very confusing to a little lad.

The girl got back in the car and the man picked me up and placed me next to her and we drove away. A traffic barrier stopped our vehicle for a while, and we had to wait for someone to raise it before we could continue our journey. I don't think we were allowed back on the beach again. (1)

I remember little of my time in this home except for there being a nearby pond and a large, flat area at the rear of the house which was referred to as a tennis court. I don't know how I was selected to stay with this family or how long I was with them.

Soon afterwards I was placed in a car and taken to another house and told I'd live there. I'd moved again, but it didn't register in my memory where I'd moved from. I'd been passed on to yet another family.

One day, I saw men and women on horseback gathering on the large, grassy area in the centre of the village. The men wore red coats, and the ladies sported long dresses and sat sidesaddle. They smiled and waved to each other while a pack of dogs sniffed and mingled around the horses, excited at the day's forthcoming activities.

A man blew a horn, and they all moved off, the dogs leading the way. The young men from the village ran alongside them shouting and waving. People threw coins at them and everyone seemed to be having fun.

I was told they were going to catch a fox over the fields and through the woods. I'd seen nothing like this before and didn't understand why all these people would want to catch a fox.

This new home lay on the border of Dorset and Devon. I don't know my age at this time, but I clearly remember the family and their way of life, which contrasted with that of the previous family. There was a big man and a big lady and two teenage girls. At first, I thought they were their daughters. The girls and I shared a room. Another man was always there too. I was told he was from another country.

The big man and his family treated me well and our school lessons took place at the house. There was plenty of food and lots of space in which to run around and play. The foreign man worked at the house and never spoke to me. Everyone referred to him as Brother and he said his prayers over and over again throughout the day.

The two girls always made my little bed and ensured I had a good wash twice a day and that I went to the toilet before bedtime. They took me by the hand for walks around the land and read me stories about gentle Jesus and all his friends.

The big man would sit me on his lap and tell me about 'the good life'. I remember this clearly; the talk always began with 'The good life...' Today, I can't remember what this good life was all about but recall that the whole family led a life of thought and prayer.

Our day began when we were awakened at, or even before, daybreak. The girls and I joined the adults downstairs for morning prayers - kneeling. Sometimes I fell asleep but was quickly awoken. The big man read aloud from a book then we sang some songs. I didn't know the words so was ignored. Afterwards he shouted orders to us all and waved his arms about. His wife, the girls, and the foreign man replied, and they all sang again. After someone had dabbed water on my forehead, they allowed me to go back to bed.

Soon one of the girls would fetch me downstairs for breakfast, for which we always thanked God, then, I was given schoolwork in the form of a puzzle, or colour recognition, and simple arithmetic. Next, we said a prayer and walked around the land for exercise and clean air. On our return we were given a bowl of something to eat then said another prayer. At this stage I was allowed a nap then, on waking, was given a book in which to draw and colour. I was told not to colour outside the lines, so I had to be careful. One of the girls would read me a nice story about little Jesus and his friends or other religious things.

Some days we all went out to the village and gave out pieces of paper with pictures of Jesus on them. I couldn't read what was written on the leaflets but noticed people throwing them away. I picked them up off the ground and gave them back to the girls. The girls were referred to as Sister 'this' or Sister 'that'. (I can't remember their names.)

As I mentioned, I was still a small lad and didn't know my age. When you leave your home at three-and-a-half and continue to move around from place to place, your date of birth is of no importance. So, what changed my happy little life?

One day, one of the sisters took me out on my daily walk. Upon our return, she was taken away by the big lady and I was sent upstairs to my room.

The big man opened my door and stepped inside, his face red. He was out of breath from climbing the stairs, and his presence frightened me.

"Where is the girl?" he asked.

"The big lady has taken her into a room down the stairs," I told him.

He turned and went back down the stairs. I heard shouting. The girl came back to our room and told me that Sister (whatever her name was) had gone away with the foreign man and she'd been told to leave as well.

She hugged me and said, "I don't want to leave you alone in the house. I'm old enough to look after you at my parents' house in Devon."

None of this made any difference to me. I'd been moved around and lived with strangers for a while. As long as I had food and a living friend it didn't bother me. I didn't see any difference.

How much time passed, I'm not sure, but the Sister returned with her mother and father. They had come to collect her and look at me.

Her father picked me up in his arms and carried me downstairs and her mother collected my belongings. They sat me beside them in the horse and trap and off we went. It was all so exciting.

The following day, the family took me to be registered as their evacuee in Appledore, a village at the mouth of the River Torridge. This was no problem as the father was a retired police officer.

Now officially living in another new home, the title 'Sister' had been dropped, and I learned the girl's name was Anne. I can't remember what her parents were called but I remember Anne's cooking, her love, and how good her father was to me.

When a child receives love and their life is full of joy and happiness, they have everything to look forward to; it was my good fortune to find all this with these country people.

Because this happened around seventy-five years ago and I was so young, I can't recall all the events they involved me in or how much fun we had together. However, one thing I remember in detail is the ingenious way Anne's father taught me arithmetic.

We began at the bottom of the stairs and he asked me to climb one stair, then another and showed me that one stair plus one stair equals two stairs because I was now standing on stair number two.

"Now come down one stair leaving one stair." I did as instructed. "So," he said, "two less one makes one because you're on stair one." I understood. "So now we go up three stairs. One, plus one, plus one makes three. Come down one stair leaving two stairs. So, three less one makes two and there are two stairs below you."

We went from three to six, from six to nine, less one or less two from three, or all the stairs leaving nil. Then he placed numbers on each stair and encouraged me to add up or take away from all the numbers.

As I learned to add and subtract, he gave me a pencil and a book to write in. Now without using the stairs, we added and subtracted from one to ten. I was a quick learner, so we no longer needed the stairs.

We sat at the table and he asked what eight stairs less three stairs was—or whatever sum came into his head. It all made sense. He made arithmetic simple and fun, and children enjoy learning much more when they're enjoying themselves.

Next, we began multiplication with the stairs, simple at first—one stair times three stairs or whatever he thought of up to two stairs times ten stairs and so on.

Next came division, although by now I was working on paper.

What a clever man, and so dedicated to teaching a small lad. He set my work out in exercise books and if I achieved ten out of ten on any exercise, he stuck a red star on the page. When I'd earned five red stars, he rewarded me with five sweets from the sweet jar.

Anne's father took me to the seaside and taught me to swim. I loved our trips to Appledore beach. The houses there were painted in various pastel shades: blue, green, pink, orange, white, and yellow, so this gave us another exercise: learning my colours. As we walked down the streets, we went through the colours and I repeated them back to him on our next visit.

When her father had to go away for a short while, Anne took charge of me and we visited a country fair at Bideford. Her mother also took me out shopping. I enjoyed this and always received a sweet or a piece of cake. Often, she baked Cornish pasties and cut one in half and I ate it before washing and getting ready for bed.

Many memories of the things we did and the places we visited have receded into the mists of time, but a damson tree comes to mind. One afternoon, I climbed up through its branches past the ripe fruit hanging amongst the leaves. Somehow, I lost my grip on the branch and came crashing down to the ground and knocked myself out. I awoke with a cold cloth on my head and to a telling off from Anne's mother.

For reasons of which I'm unaware, I was moved on from this home. I don't think I'd done anything wrong. Maybe they had another child moving in and my time there was up. Anne's mother took me on a bus. This adventure was over, and I was on my way to a new home.

I later discovered that many evacuees were moved around from home to home without the permission of the authorities. Some, like me, got lost from the system. Most of the men were fighting for our country and so the high work-load of inexperienced workers, and short-staffed departments, only served to compound this problem.

I arrived at a place called Wing in Buckinghamshire. All I remember about the move was that it was a long way from the home I'd settled into and the friends I had made. Another WVS lady collected me and drove me along a country road. I looked out of the window and watched the hedges, trees, and fields passing by. We stopped outside a house. The lady helped me out of the vehicle, and I stood by her side as she knocked on the door.

It opened, and a big lady with a huge red face and smile scooped me up, kissed, and hugged me, then took me inside the house. It was warm and had a lovely smell. She sat me on her knee and hugged and kissed me over and over. I must have been in shock at all this attention. I put my arms around the lady and wouldn't let go. I was in heaven and wanted this to go on forever.

Immediately, I came under the big lady's spell. She was warm and everything a little lad needed—how lucky I was again. This was my sixth or seventh home since leaving my parents; I'd lost count.

She showed me the bed upstairs where I'd sleep. At night, I snuggled under the warm blankets and let my head sink into the soft pillow. The lady had two grown daughters, one of whom lived with her, but no boys. My new home had no electricity or gas and no running water. The rainwater ran off the roof, along the guttering, and down pipes where it collected in a large barrel at the side of the house. At twilight, oil lamps were lit in the downstairs rooms, but we used candles upstairs. Cooking was done in a large, black, cast-iron oven powered by an internal fire, and each room had a fireplace fuelled by wood, which we collected from the fields and lanes all around us. Water was boiled on the oven. My marvelous, new carer cooked food inside and on top of the oven, and the smell of homemade bread and pies often filled that little three-bed roomed house.

Nature's call was answered with a walk down the path to a small brick shed where the toilet comprised a wooden seat. All waste fell into a large, straw-filled bin doused with copious amounts of disinfectant. When this filled, the big lady dragged it out onto a wheeled trolley and pulled it down the lane at the rear of the house. Here, she dumped it into a large hole followed by more disinfectant, straw, and earth. It wasn't a pleasant job, especially in summertime, but one got used to it.

I was too small to help, but the big lady, Mrs Plumbridge, was strong, and would carry me under one arm whilst pushing the bin down to the hole. She always gave me several kisses and what she called a sandpaper rub with her knuckles on the top of my head.

I was happy, contented and felt secure. My life was everything a little lad could wish for. I was loved and lived in a warm home with nutritious, homemade food. Soon, I was enrolled in and began attending the village school. I didn't need to follow the roadway to get there; I walked or ran across the large buttercup field beside our house. Sharing village life with rural people was a wonderful experience. They had plenty of time for children and never stopped helping them with their education in life... what a lucky little lad I was.

1. Because of the low population density of nearby areas and their proximity to the naval base on Portland, before and during World War II the RAF used Chesil beach as an experimental bombing range. It was also used for machine gun training and highball bouncing bomb testing. We had come across the men of the armed forces training before going out on manoeuvres. War experts had predicted the Germans might use Chesil beach for an invasion, so defensive measures were undertaken along the twenty-six-mile-long beach including installing anti-tank blocks, digging an anti-tank ditch, constructing admiralty scaffolding and pillboxes, and setting minefields—both on land and under the sea. Pillboxes were fortified concrete or stone structures built around twelve feet long. Soldiers could stand inside them and fire at the advancing enemy through narrow slits.

Chapter 3

Harvest Time

I have no clear idea of how old I was at this time or how long I spent with my wonderful Mrs Plumbridge. We went for walks in the evenings and she taught me about the different types of trees, their names, and for what the wood was used. I could name wild flowers and knew which were poisonous, all because Mrs Plumbridge taught me. She knew where the badger setts were, and we often watched the large animals running about the hillsides and under the trees with their black and white striped faces. She pointed out foxes and rabbits, and different types of birds, telling me their names.

Mrs Plumbridge showed me how to catch rabbits and could dispatch one in seconds. When she wanted to cook a rabbit or make a pie, we would walk out and come back with at least two rabbits.

When I first came to stay in the country, I was upset when the rabbits were killed, but she took me on her knee and explained, "Mr Fox will eat them if we don't, and the farmer will put poison down their burrows and they will suffer painful deaths."

I nodded; glad the rabbits wouldn't suffer. I reasoned, *the more we catch the better it will be for the rabbits*. They still didn't have much of a chance, but we had Mr Fox's dinner at least once a week.

The seasons controlled the way of life in the country. This was clear by the number of hours the farmers and their helpers worked at different times of the year, and there were no weekends off. Despite the long hours and hard work, they enjoyed what they did. This way of life was part of their being, bred into them from generations past.

When the country folk asked a question, it was usually about the land or the weather. Most of the farming wives always kept a sweet in whatever large bag they were carrying and always referred to me as 'the little evacuee lad'. They often mentioned that I needed feeding up, so it went through my head we had to catch more rabbits.

The fields at the front and rear of our little house were full of wheat and at harvest time along came the tractors followed by men with guns to shoot the rabbits as they ran out of the uncut crop.

Labourers and other helpers tied the bundles of cut wheat together and stacked them into something called stands, which were made of six bundles of tied wheat. Each work day began around 7 am. This work was hard and had to be completed quickly, so no-one went home until after 9 pm.

As the wheat was harvested, the rabbits ran for their lives towards the shooters who were waiting for them. Guns fired, and rabbits stopped in their tracks, hit by the shots that echoed down the valley. The dead rabbits were promptly bagged. I'd been given the job of pushing the bundles of wheat together and making sure that no rabbits ran inside them to hide from the guns.

For a little lad it was very exciting: the sweet, powdery smell of freshly cut wheat, the crack of the guns and the acrid smell of spent gun powder, the roar of the tractors engine, the sight of balers stacking wheat and running from place to place—sweating as they lugged the bales and threw them on top of the stands—rabbits running for their lives, men calling to each other, children running around in the hot sunshine.

At midday, the farm ladies appeared on a flatbed trailer with homemade bread, sausages, cheese, pickles, cider, milk, and jugs of water for everybody in the field. The shooters handed over their rabbits, and the labourers stopped working for thirty minutes, (which generally stretched to about an hour) such was the feast sent from the farm.

Mrs Plumbridge was in the thick of things from the start. I sat with her in the shade of the hedge for a midday rest and munched on freshly baked bread with butter and cheese and drank a cup of milk—all produced at the farm and all delicious, with an added kiss and cuddle from Mrs Plumbridge.

The following evening, we were invited to the farmhouse for dinner: rabbit pie with red cabbage and new potatoes followed by baked apple from the orchard. I remember the farm wives' words 'you need to feed him up, your evacuee'. I had everything I could wish for, a good home, good people, a school I enjoyed, and food lords and ladies would die for, but there was another bonus coming my way... a special memory I would cherish all my life.

Chapter 4

My Sweetheart

It was a warm summer's evening, and I was enjoying my walk home from school across the buttercup field. I looked up and followed the flight of a House Martin as it flew across the blue sky towards the farm outbuildings. Suddenly, I heard a noise behind me. I looked around. I wanted to run but my legs felt weak. My heart raced.

A sand-coloured horse towered above me. It had followed me across the field. I stood rooted to the spot, staring at it through wide-open eyes. The horse stood still looking at me with its head bobbing up and down. Finally able to move, I made a run for the fence near the house. The horse ran alongside me matching my pace. When I stopped, the horse stopped and walked towards me pausing two or three feet away, still nodding its head. (Horses will only do this if they feel safe and secure with you.)

I crept towards the fence and the horse walked beside me. I looked at it and felt the urge to pat it on the side, so I did, and it stood still with its head bobbing up and down and its tail swishing about. Its coat was so soft. My fear had gone. I grinned the biggest grin. How wonderful was this? The horse was so tall I could run underneath its belly through its strong, stocky legs. This was our first meeting, and we were in love. I got no kisses from the horse but the two big eyes looking at me underneath its yellow mane were enough to melt my heart.

I ran into the kitchen, grabbed some carrots, then ran back to the field and climbed onto the fence. The horse lifted its head and opened its mouth and crunched all my carrots.

Mrs Plumbridge spotted me from the small kitchen window and came out into the rear garden. "Don, I've given permission for the horse to live in the field. It needs to rest." She smiled and looked over the fence at my new friend. "It's a Suffolk Punch, but is bigger than they usually are." Mrs Plumbridge had known the horse for about two years and it had been very well looked after by a local farmer. "You mustn't be frightened by such a big, strong animal," she added. "It won't do you any harm. You should spend some time with it."

(Because of the Suffolk Punch's strong frame and thick rump, farmers often used this breed to pull heavy items.)

The horse was called Peter. He stayed by the fence for several hours, and once I'd eaten my tea, made my bed, and cleaned my boots, I was allowed to take some cabbage, carrots, and grain in a tin pan and slide it underneath the fence to feed him.

We soon formed a special relationship. He waited for me night and day. When I set off for school, he was waiting by the fence for a tit-bit. On school days I ran into the garden, and after cuddling its huge head, I climbed through the bars of the fence and we walked or ran across the field. He stood and watched me until I disappeared into the school.

When the home-time school bell rang, he trotted over and we walked home across the buttercup field together. When I ran Peter ran. If I stopped and turned the other way so did Peter. He loved to play, always with his head bobbing up and down, up and down.

One evening, I climbed on top of the fence and tried to climb onto Peter's back. This didn't work as his back was too wide for my little legs. I was determined to ride that horse so tried again and again. Eventually, Mrs Plumbridge saw what I was doing and solved the problem.

She lifted me up and placed me on Peter's huge neck with one of my legs on each side. "Hold tight to his mane and keep your knees tight to his neck. When his head comes up move to one side or you'll be hit."

Peter walked away from the fence. I was in another world as high as when I climbed a tree, but this was better. I could feel the warmth of his back on my legs and his muscles moving around beneath me. For a moment I was frightened of falling to the ground, but Mrs Plumbridge walked next to me to catch me if I fell from Peter's neck. He was gentle and didn't move quickly. Soon, I gained confidence and relaxed. We walked round and round amongst the long grass and wild flowers until Mrs Plumbridge pulled my leg and I slipped down into her arms.

I soon learned to climb onto Peter's neck from the fence with no help. I would grip his mane and off we went. If I pushed my knees into his neck, he'd break into a trot. I learnt to ride as I'd seen the fox-hunters in red coats doing when they crossed our field. In the mornings we would have a few trots around the field before I climbed onto the fence and after a head cuddle went into school. Peter would watch me all the way and sometimes would push the turf up with a hoof or make a snorting noise through his big nose. I always gave him a wave, and sometimes he'd stay there for hours without moving.

A teacher at the school saw my 'Wild West Show' and asked me if I'd show the class my skill at home-time, so at 4 pm we all walked to the fence. After a moment Peter joined us. The other children stepped back from the fence, scared by his size and power.

I climbed the horizontal slats of the fence, jumped onto his neck, and off we trotted across the field. When I pulled Peter's mane to the left, he turned left and likewise when I pulled it to the right he turned right.

I sat tall on his neck, a huge grin on my face. Two or three teachers, several more pupils and the escorts who took them home, joined the crowd and watched our show. After a few gallops around the field Peter and I headed back to the side of the field where our audience clapped in enjoyment.

When I got home, I told Mrs Plumbridge about my exhibition and as normal I received a big kiss. She was proud of me. I was the son she never had. What a lucky lad I was.

My life was so good and full of excitement. I was growing fast and outgrew my clothes every few weeks. On Saturdays we took the bus to the market in Leighton Buzzard where Mrs Plumbridge purchased second hand boys' clothes and boots. I didn't own a pair of shoes, underpants, or vests until I was fourteen.

One day at school, someone told the children to form a queue to see the school doctor. While we were waiting in the corridor, the teacher told us all to strip down to our underwear. I had none, so the teacher allowed me to wear my short, grey trousers, and socks. He commented that I was an evacuee from somewhere and that's why I didn't have underwear.

At home, that evening, I told Mrs Plumbridge and the next day she appeared at the school, found the teacher, and in front of the class informed him I had no parents she knew of.

"Showing a young lad up like that is a disgrace," she said. "He won't be coming back to school again."

She took me home and gave me a large cup of tea and a slice of cake, and I never went back to that school. This gave me more time to spend with Peter, which suited both of us. Our rides got longer and longer, and we fell asleep together in the buttercup field on more than one occasion. I even smelt like a horse.

Chapter 5

Not a Good Mile

Not long after the school incident, a man appeared at our little house wearing an overcoat and carrying a black bag. He asked me various questions I can't remember now, then looked upstairs and downstairs, inspected the toilet down the path, and examined the rainwater barrel which was our water supply. He took his hat and disappeared up the lane on his bike.

Within days, a policeman who knew Mrs Plumbridge arrived and informed her he'd to remove me from her care. The man in the overcoat had submitted an official report condemning the house as unfit.

After an exchange of words, the policeman left on his bike looking miserable and irate. Mrs Plumbridge came back in the living room in tears. I stood by her wanting to make her feel better, but I didn't know how. She saw my distress and promised no one would take me away. All this had come about because of her school visit and my removal from the school.

It wasn't long before a car arrived at the house and a policeman knocked on the door accompanied by two other men. Paperwork was displayed, and I was ordered to put my things in a bag (I didn't have enough to fill a bag anyway) and go to the car.

All hell let loose—which was very frightening. One man ended up on his back outside on the path, the policeman's hat was on the floor, and the other man was still trying to present the papers which were now in shreds. They didn't realise how strong the lady was both in physique and will-power. Round one to Mrs. Plumbridge. The men got in their car and drove away.

It was all to no avail; I was removed. Mrs Plumbridge let me go but was heartbroken and screamed and chased the car all the way up the lane. I withdrew into myself and didn't talk for weeks. I'd lost my home, my beautiful Peter, my beloved guardian and teacher. My heart was broken, my life, my security, my will to live had been torn from me. Why had this happened? What had I done?

Everything I loved had gone because a man in a large overcoat with a big bag had said so. This was the end of a chapter for me and for all the people involved with my life. I'd been happy, well cared for, and loved, which was everything a young lad needed to grow up healthy and well-adjusted. To snatch me away from this life was disgraceful. I hadn't believed it would happen... but it did, and I was alone again.

Someone drove me to a boys' home in Buckinghamshire, called Ivinghoe. I remember there being a large hill in the middle of a nearby field known as Ivinghoe Beacon.

The boys' home was overcrowded. I shared a room with eight or ten other lads sleeping two in a bunk, top to tail. Again, I was allocated a bottom bunk.

What was I doing here? What had I done to be moved to this place?

I became angry and aggressive and had fight after fight with the other boys. The sweet little boy was gone; I was like an animal. Consequently, I was removed from the house and made to sleep in the outside shed. It suited me to be alone, but it was like a prison and cold at night and hot during the day.

I'm not sure how long they kept me in the shed. They couldn't let me out as I would have run away back to my life with Peter and my wonderful Mrs Plumbridge—if I could have found my way back to her little house in Wing.

Someone enrolled me at the village school across the road from the home. I remember there being a maypole with ribbons in every colour at the side of the school and the children dancing around it at holiday time.

I wasn't interested in dancing around a pole and had never heard of holidays. Nothing held any interest for me. I was surviving in my own little world, which was fine as long as everyone left me alone and I could return to my shed, lie on the bed and stare at the wooden roof. I hated the men with black briefcases, overcoats, and papers. There was no way of venting this hate, so it boiled up inside, but I didn't cry.

After a time, I was moved from my shed to a room somewhere in the grounds to live with a lady who spoke a funny language. She was a refugee from another country and worked at the boys' home as a cook. Occasionally, a few of her words sounded like English, but the rest of the time she warbled on and on without a break. I didn't see how she'd time to take a breath.

Every morning, she left our room early to cook breakfast at the home but always came to wake me up, say a prayer, and give me a cup of tea, and sometimes bread, sausages, and porridge. She was a good woman. I learned many years later that she was a German Jew. All her family had been killed, and the only reason she was in England was that a sum of money had been paid to Germany for her freedom. She'd lost everything but never once complained.

Over the time I spent with her, I learnt some of her language: 'schnell' was quick, 'nein' was no, 'ja' was yes, and 'auf wiedersehen' was goodbye. 'Guten tag' meant good day, and 'guten abend' meant good evening. I also learned to count to twenty in German.

She knitted me a woollen hat, gloves, and a scarf. She could never be a Mrs Plumbridge, but she came a close second and showed me genuine love.

I don't know how long I stayed at Ivinghoe, but one day an official appeared asking questions. I had a feeling I was on the move again and that is exactly what happened.

I was told to report to the supervisor's office and some days after being questioned by yet another fool with an overcoat and briefcase, a recommendation was put forward that I be sent to a new home.

My stay with the Jewish lady had got me back on track, and we both cried when I had to leave. Over time, I grew out of the knitwear she made me, but I kept it safe to remind me of her, and I still have a toy she made me out of the lining of an overcoat. I have fond memories of our friendship and her name recently came into my mind: Hanna Reich—although I'm not sure of the spelling.

The toy, a small Tiger stuffed with old clothes, still stands to this day in a bedroom in my house. A little worse for wear for being played with by my daughter when she was small, it remains a constant reminder of the friendship Hanna and I shared over 75 years ago.

I often wonder what happened to her. Did she go back to Germany or did she find love and marry in Buckinghamshire? We were two misfits thrown together, swept up by events over which we had no control—A little Lad and a Jewish refugee.

Chapter 6

Goodbye to Buckinghamshire

Off I went to another home, this time in Middlesex. After a long journey, I was taken into a room where there were lots of men and told to wait for the bus.

It didn't take long for the room to empty. I sat there alone wondering where I'd go next and with whom I'd be living. A WVS lady arrived and off we went. Her voice was gentle, and she'd lots of kind words and told me how nice it was where I was going.

I ended up in Feltham. Bit by bit I was moving around England and each time a different WVS lady assured me how nice it would be at my new home.

When we arrived at the house, a man opened the front door dressed in a fireman's uniform. His wife was a small, dark-skinned lady. They had two children—a daughter three years older than me and a son around three years old.

When all the introductions had been carried out, the WVS lady left. She'd done her bit for the war effort that day. All the volunteer ladies were very nice and always had sweets to give out. By now, I'd become used to new homes, new people, new beds, different ways of life, and how everything changed after a short time.

I found it easy to settle into this new home. Sometimes people asked me how old I was. I didn't know. I didn't even know which month I'd been born or my date of birth. Birthdays and such things held no meaning to me, they didn't exist in my little world. Food and warmth summed up my needs, everything else had been stolen away bit by bit by the men who moved me about like a toy.

I settled into the house in Feltham and slowly began to communicate with the daughter and her school friends who came around dressed in their school uniforms. The mother was a very hard-working woman. I didn't see much of the father. He was out fighting fires most of the time.

At the end of the extensive, rear garden was a shed. It contained all kinds of equipment to aid in the cultivation of vegetables and fruit and to keep their large, white ducks, banty hens, a rooster, several rabbits, and a miniature pig. That pig loved being scratched under its chin or rubbed down its back with a yard-brush.

Everything at the rear of the house was there to support the family. They grew food to feed themselves and sold produce to their neighbours. The parents showed me how to feed the hens and clean them out and how to keep the ducks away from the rooster. I was told to hit it with a stick if it came after my legs. That rooster was a terror. It woke the whole row of houses up every morning with its 'cock-a-doodle-doo'.

I collected the hen and duck eggs every morning and cleaned the pens out once a week. Duck eggs are bigger than hen eggs so I couldn't mix them up.

The pig was white with black, dappled patches on his body and head. It was my job to let him out with a rope around his neck and take him to the wooded area at the back of the houses to root around in the grass and undergrowth. If he got off his rope, he'd run like the wind everywhere, round and round in circles, so he'd to be watched with great attention.

Once, he fell down a hole, and it took two firemen several hours to dig him out. The pig was allowed indoors too and loved to lie by the fire in the kitchen, but should he twitch his nose and shake his back leg he was quickly put back in his shed. This warning sign meant he was about to break wind, and you wouldn't want to be down wind of him when he did that.

I named the little pig 'Stink' and spent much of my time feeding, washing, scratching, and walking him. He loved being around me which caused a few problems when I tried to get him back into his shed. He knew I was going to leave him there so tried everything to avoid going back inside it.

A small crowd of boys gathered around me in the school yard as I told them all about Stink and pleaded with me to bring him to the school fair on a Saturday. I agreed as long as they would help me get him in the wheelbarrow because he couldn't walk all the way to school. It was too far for his little legs.

On the chosen Saturday, two boys arrived, at the house. We padded the wheelbarrow with straw and grass and placed a bunch of carrots in there, and, after a lot of heaving and panting, we got Stink into the barrow.

He'd never been in the wheelbarrow before but loved it. I secured his rope to the handles to stop him jumping out, and we set off up the road towards the School.

Stink was in his element being wheeled around the streets. Children and parents patted him and fed him cake, bread, and carrots etc. He sat on his straw lapping up the attention with the occasional grunt and a sniff of the air.

By the time we arrived at the school playground, Stink had fallen asleep in his straw-lined wheelbarrow and was passing lots of wind and snoring.

Living through a war had a psychological impact on many, especially the vulnerable. People living in cities lived in a constant state of fear. They didn't know if they would wake up in the morning or if their houses would be bombed out. Some lived in fear of receiving a telegram or a knock on the door by the local policeman telling them their sons or husband had been killed or were missing in action. For years to come this would have a profound effect on society and individuals. People needed a pleasant distraction for a few hours, hence the school Open Days.

Children brought along pet rabbits, dogs, cats, and a crazy variety of other animals, but there were no other pigs. Stink was the first.

He was an immediate success and sat upright in his barrow playing the crowd. Parents and children laughed and pointed at him when they spotted him. We lifted him out of the barrow and, keeping him on a tight lead, wandered off to see the stalls. It amazed me how much time and money had gone into preparing the exhibits. One stall was full of handmade dolls of all shapes, sizes, and designs, and, if you wished, you could buy glass eyes, hair, and cloth for stuffing, and make your own.

Stink noticed a stuffed toy pig on display and tried to snuffle up to it with his snout but then got a sniff of the food on the next stall and lost interest in the toy.

The army cadets, all of whom attended the school, were out on parade, showing everybody how to march, and the Land Army girls arrived with a large tractor and lots of freshly grown farm produce promoting their work by handing out leaflets to the crowd. Their part in the war effort was vital.

Still holding Stinks' rope, I walked past a group of boy scouts and over to the coconut-shy stall. I don't think they were real coconuts—these would have been hard to come by during wartime—but the stall was making plenty of money from the local 'jack the lads' who were taking turns throwing wooden balls at the coconuts to impress the young ladies.

A small band of sea cadets (again, youngsters attending the school) struck up on the far side of the playing field. Stink was not interested in any of this activity. He just kept sniffing the air on the lookout for more food.

Across the field we noticed a Pedigree Dog Show taking place. The owners were leading their dogs around in a circle while a lady stood in the middle marking papers. This was our chance to have fun. My friends encouraged me to slip into the pen with Stink and walk around as though he were a dog, and so I did.

The crowd went wild with laughter, but the lady Judge was not amused. All the while, Stink continued to pass more wind.

None of the commotion bothered him, he rolled over and scratched his back on the grass with his legs in the air.

A teacher from the Upper school noticed the commotion and strode across the field. She glared at me, then stink and then at me again, and asked us to leave so the officials could continue with their judging. Some people have no sense of humour.

I tried, but Stink wasn't for moving. He was still rolling on his back on the grass having a lovely time. After a lot of effort, I rolled him over and got him back on his feet. I think he was a little put out because he didn't get a pat on the back from the Judges like the other dogs.

The interfering teacher told me to report to the Headmaster on Monday morning. I was in trouble, but it didn't bother me. I was only having a little fun. Our joining in the dog show did no harm and a lot of spectators seemed to enjoy the silly episode.

I saw the day as a complete success for Stink, except for one slight mishap. The little pig had eaten bits of this and that all day, which was asking for trouble. He slowly edged closer to a stall where a lady was buying chutney, and when she reached over to pay, he emptied his bowels on her foot. To say she was not happy was an understatement.

There was a lot going on that Open Day and my friends and I enjoyed being there, but by mid-afternoon I found I needed to pull harder on Stink's rope to get him to walk with me. This was his way of telling me he was getting tired. My friends and I grabbed hold of him around the belly and heaved and pushed him back into the wheelbarrow. People had fed him tit-bits all day, so as soon as he felt the softness of the straw beneath him, he fell fast asleep and began snoring... all the while his leg shaking as he produced even more wind.

With a little help from my pals, I wheeled Stink home and within seconds he was fast asleep in his shed, his legs twitching as he continued breaking wind. He was probably dreaming of more food.

I had many other experiences with Stink. Once he dug a large hole under his shed and wandered into it to sleep for two days. When he needed to eat and drink, he came out covered in mud. I washed him down with a hosepipe and cleaned him with the yard-brush. He loved this and rolled on his back and showed me his belly. What a little show off he was. I could go on and on about Stink.

His best friend was the cat from next door, who, on occasions, would climb over the fence and sleep with him at night. They would cuddle up together in the straw, the cat licking Stink's ears. If I went near them, the cat would growl and hiss at me, thinking he was protecting Stink.

I'm not too sure what that cat was called or if it was a tom or a queen; it was a big over-fed black and white thing, always digging up the carrots and scratching around in the garden.

Whenever Stink was out in the garden the cat would appear and jump on his back. When the little pig became too excited, or if he twitched his nose and shook his back leg, the cat would leap off him and onto the safety of the fence. Even he recognised this imminent warning sign of Stink's intention to break wind.

That cat had belonged to the local farm but had made next door its home some years before and was not for moving. Since Stink had arrived as a tiny piglet, it had never left his side. They shared a bond that went back many years. It was I who was the intruder.

The lady from next door loved Stink almost as much as I did and would even allow him in her kitchen. There were always fun and games whenever Stink tried to lie down in the cat's basket, as he'd done when he was a little piglet. By now, he was too big to fit so would give up and flop down on the floor in front of the fire, and the cat would lie on top of him.

I enjoyed my involvement with the garden/small farm and spent most of the time when not at school either tending the livestock or growing vegetables in the rear garden: potatoes, lettuce, onions, beetroot, runner beans, cabbage, Brussels sprouts, and, in the summer months, strawberries, gooseberries and black and red-currants. The main enemy was slugs. If their numbers were not kept in check, they would eat the produce so, as there were no slug pellets around in those days, I had to sprinkle salt over the vegetables. Slugs hated this and wouldn't go near it. Stink did his part too, eating one or two of the slugs and stamping on the rest. This was like being back with Mrs Plumbridge and sometimes my mind drifted back to the vegetables we had tended together. I didn't dwell on the memory of my removal from her home, but I still longed to be back with her.

***

Many years later, while on business with one of my staff at a company outside Leighton Buzzard, a market town near Wing, I took a detour to find the house I'd lived in with Mrs Plumbridge.

I soon located it and parked my car in the road outside. The house seemed much smaller than I remembered. Memories of Peter galloping across the buttercup field flooded back. I couldn't find it in me to approach the house but got out of the car and leaned on the fence. In my mind's eye I could see Mrs Plumbridge working in her garden. I didn't knock on the door or stay long; the feelings I had were unhappy in one respect and yet wonderful in another. It was like clutching at something long gone but that wouldn't go away.

I took a deep breath and got back in my car, stopping at a local public house for a drink and a sandwich. I was in no hurry so got talking to a local man around my own age. He'd lived in the area all his life and remembered Mrs Plumbridge but not me. What he told me was to leave yet more hurt. Sometime after my removal, his late mother and Mrs Plumbridge had obtained paperwork of some description hoping to find her young evacuee and have him returned to her care.

I don't know where they searched for me as I'd been moved to Middlesex. This, again, showed the depth of love that wonderful lady had for a little boy who had no home or friends, apart from Peter the horse. In our short time together, we shared something special and no official with pieces of paper backed up by the police could ever take that away.

I have never forgotten the love this amazing, farming lady, Mrs Plumbridge showed me. Neither have I forgotten the invaluable life lessons I learned and the time we shared. Although it was short, and I wished it could have lasted much longer, it's indelibly imprinted in my memory. I am truly thankful for all the love I received and the memories that are still so warm in my mind.

The traumatic ereption from this near perfect home taught me a lesson that helped shape my business life. I now treat with suspicion the Brigade of Officials that appear from the woodwork with information and directives. These usually mean I have to change direction or spend money, so I always get a second opinion before taking any action. The men with the black overcoats never change and never will.

Chapter 7

Prisoners of War

Back in Feltham, my life was about to become eventful.

One Saturday afternoon I was happily swinging on the gate at the front of the house when I heard a noise. I looked up the road to my left. The noise became louder and louder and I saw two British solders walking towards me carrying rifles. Behind them were dozens of soldiers, some sang and waved. I continued watching them march past. Many had bloody bandages wrapped around their heads, arms, and legs, and some wore long, green overcoats. The ones without coats wore dirty, ripped uniforms like battle-weary men fresh from the battlefield. All these were unarmed. More British soldiers, all carrying rifles, marched with them on each side of the road. The injured men were German Prisoners of War.

A few shouted across to me in German and some waved their hats. I remembered a few words Hanna had taught me when I lived with her at Ivinghoe and shouted back 'Guten Tag' (Good Day) and waved back to them. One or two shouted a greeting in German and ran over to my gate. They must have thought I was a little German boy. The British soldiers took this the wrong way and struck them on their heads and backs with their rifles. Already weakened by their injuries, some fell onto the hard ground. The British soldiers ran to their sides, pointed their bayonets at them, and shouted words a small boy should never hear. Eventually, things calmed down, and they all marched on again. I realised I'd been greeted by German soldiers covered in dirt and blood, and all of them had a foul smell. I was petrified. I jumped off the gate and ran to the shed at the back of the house where I sat with Stink for a while, my heart racing, then took him for a walk.

Sometimes on our walks we came into contact with other soldiers who wore diamond patches on their backs and trouser legs. These Italian Prisoners of War were employed on the farms. They were always cheerful and spoke in a 'sing song' language. I let them stroke Stink and he certainly seemed to like them so that was okay for me.

One evening there was trouble outside the cinema. The reason appears to have been because some Italian POW's had been refused entry.

However, it was the girls who accompanied them who were getting fired up not the men. The whole thing seemed strange as the POW's were laughing and full of fun, singing in their mother tongue and not at all bothered about going into the cinema. When all the shouting had stopped, they went on their way, still singing, the girls following them.

I told the lady I lived with what happened outside the cinema.

"The POWs won't understand the films anyway," she said. "They're all in English." She told me that some POWs had been removed from the cinema the previous week because the one who spoke English was translating the film to his pals in Italian. He spoke a little too loudly and this disturbed everyone else in the picture house. No one could follow the film. The manager had asked the POW's to leave and had refunded them their money.

From then on, the manager's rule was that all the Italian POW's were to be refused entry unless they could speak English fluently.

The people I lived with in Feltham had a tandem with a small seat on the back for their little son and a single bike for their daughter. The object of their having me stay with them was for me to look after the livestock, garden, and house whilst they went off cycling from Friday until Sunday evenings.

I was pleased to be left on my own with the gardening and Stink. The ducks and banty hens roamed about on their own so I only needed to gather the eggs. It gave me a sense of importance to be in charge of everything, and the shed at the end of the garden was my little home where I sold the eggs to regular customers. At the end of each day I placed the money in a tin and hid it in our hiding-place inside the piano in the front room.

On one such weekend, I sold eggs to two ladies and overheard part of their conversation as they walked away. One remarked to the other that not only did the people I live with have a free servant, they also had my ration book and were being paid by the government to look after me. Only many years later did I understand the full meaning of what I'd overheard.

Another Saturday, after I'd finished looking after the livestock and had locked my shed, I went to the next-door neighbour's house for tea. She was living on her own, so I was company for those few hours.

When it was time for me to leave, she walked back with me and came inside the house and waited until I'd locked the back door. I had a wash and went off to bed and dropped off to sleep.

A while later, I was awakened by lots of noise coming from downstairs. I didn't know how late it was, but it was dark outside. I climbed out of bed and went down to the kitchen.

The table had been dragged over to the left, which was probably what had woken me, and a man was standing on it with his back to me. He was busy emptying the high-level cupboards of their contents.

I walked around the table and looked up at him. He looked down at me and froze. We stared at each other for what seemed a long time, then he climbed down to the floor and asked me who I was.

"I'm the evacuee from Buckinghamshire. I lived with Mrs Plumbridge and Peter the horse before this."

His eyes darted around the kitchen and steeled back to me. "Where did you come from?"

"Upstairs."

"We can play a game together if you want to." I nodded. "It's called 'finding money'."

I grinned and took him into the front room, opened the piano, and showed him the money I'd taken from selling eggs.

"Great," he said, tipping the coins into his hands and dropping them into his pocket. "We can play another game now called 'cleaning all the door knobs'."

I fetched some cloths, and we cleaned around the rooms and rubbed all the door knobs. Then we rubbed all the tins and bottles he'd removed from the cupboards. He said we were dancing around like fairies. After the kitchen table had been put back, and the tins and bottles put away, the game was over.

"I have to be back in fairyland before it gets light," he said, giving me a penny. "This is our secret. You can't tell anyone about my visit to earth." He left by the back door. I locked it and went back to bed, pleased I'd played with a real fairy. I think I was around six years old at this point, although I cannot be certain of my true age.

The people I lived with arrived home as usual on the Sunday evening. They sent me to my room so I could have enough sleep and be up for school the following morning. I'd forgotten about the fairy visiting me in the middle of the night.

On Monday morning, I went to school as usual but had not been in the classroom long when two policemen arrived asking for me. They drove me home in a police car and took me in the house. The fireman with whom I was living was red in the face and speaking in a strange language. (He was Welsh). His wife was crying.

He turned to face me and shouted. My heart raced and I couldn't speak. He began pushing and shoving me around. The policemen did nothing at first, but when the fireman grabbed my shoulder and began shaking me one of them stepped in and tried to calm things down. The other asked me questions about the loss of the household money.

I told them the fairy had taken it in the night and showed them the penny he'd given me. The Welshman's face grew redder. He stared at me through wide-open eyes. I noticed the spittle building up in the corners of his mouth as he shouted. He brought back his arm and struck me across the head. His wife tried to shield me, but the fireman was stronger. The policemen had to step in. I was dizzy with fear and my legs felt weak, but I refused to cry.

For my protection, one of them gently took my arm and led me back to the police car.

The police wanted to know why I was left in the house on my own over the weekends. I tightened my grip around the penny the fairy had given me and stared back at them. They were concerned. Being alone didn't bother me at all. I had the livestock and my little friend, Stink, for company.

The 'fairy theft' episode opened a large can of worms for the family, but, for me, that was the end of Feltham, the garden, and my friendship with Stink. The 'fairy', I later learned, was a young man in his twenties. He'd escaped from a detention centre and was also absent without leave from the army.

Some very nice ladies in green uniforms visited me at the police station and took me to a nearby pond. I remember them calling themselves 'Land Girls' and telling me they were away from home too. They said I might be allowed to go with them to the farm where they worked, as the police had told them I liked animals, but that didn't happen, and I never saw them again.

Chapter 8

The war intensifies

After being removed from Feltham I went to various places, I don't recall where, but I know one place was near a park. I remember standing with other people and they were all looking up at a funny grey aeroplane. It had short wings, made a put put put noise like a tractor and was stooping, that is, aiming downwards. Suddenly, it changed direction.

Someone gasped, and a woman screamed, "It's coming down, run, run!"

Everyone ran in all directions. I didn't know what the panic was about, but I ran as fast as I could. The aeroplane nosedived and crashed onto a row of houses. What I witnessed was too horrific to recall or write here. I had seen a strike by a V1 flying bomb, a 'doodlebug', as they were called, and I didn't want to be near one again.

I ran to my new home and through shock and gasps for breath related what I'd seen and the devastation it caused. The lady of the house began to cry. Her husband had been cycling home from work a few weeks previously and had been blown off his bike through a large shop window. He'd died instantly. (2)

Such happenings were now an everyday event. The following day there was another explosion in the street. The milk lady (all the milkmen had gone to war) had been saved from injury by sheltering inside a red phone box. Unfortunately, the horse attached to the milk cart had been killed and the shattered glass bottles blown all over the road and the poor horse. The milk dripped off the fences, shrubs, and pooled on the road.

A few days later I was in the park with some lads when I heard the dreaded put put put sound again directly above me. I watched the grey plane circle around and the put put put sound suddenly stopped.

The world slowed down and played in slow motion. The grey plane came down flat, not in a dive, and landed in front of us. It skimmed along the grass then slowed, and, as one of its wings dragged the earthy ground, it twisted in a circular path and came to a standstill. And that was that. No explosion. Nothing.

We ran for our lives. Whilst we hid behind a large tree waiting for the explosion, a policeman turned up, riding a bike, and told us to move away, quickly.

I don't know what happened afterwards, but I'll never forget the image of that grey rocket, skimming along the grass full of death and destruction.

After leaving Feltham, I spent a short time in a rough part of London. Gangs of young men competed for territory even though much of the district had been devastated by bombing.

While the authorities found me a home, I temporarily lived in a hostel where a lady supported me. One day someone asked me to go to the local shop for a packet of Woodbine cigarettes. In those days children could do this. I set off, the money in my pocket.

As I walked along the street, I noticed a mob of boys hanging around outside the shop. One of them, a tall lad, said something to me. I didn't hear him clearly, so I asked him what he'd said. He took a shiny thing from his pocket. There was a click and a long blade appeared. He lunged forward pointing the blade towards me. I raised my hand to protect myself and yelled as red-hot pain seared my arm. He'd cut me and left a six-inch wound running down from my elbow. It was so deep I saw the yellow bone before the blood spattered out. Two men rushed out of the shop and took control. The police arrived, and I was taken to the hospital for stitches, then on to the Police Station for questioning. To this day, I have a long scar down my arm.

By the time I arrived, the police had arrested the boy who had stabbed me, and he was at the police station with his father. Once the father saw how small I was he punched his son in the face and body. The police did nothing to stop him.

The older lad had just come out of Borstal, a remand home for violent youths. Sometime later his father came to me and asked me to forgive his son. He asked about my home and my parents and was upset when I couldn't give him any information. He visited me at the hostel several times. The staff there told me he was a docker and lived a few streets away in the Guinness Flats. He was kind, and I visited him several times for Sunday dinner and sometimes for my tea, usually with winkles. The son had been taken away after the attack and I never saw him again.

I later discovered the lad had asked me, 'Do you want to bleed rust?' (Gang-speak for 'I am going to stab you'... which he did.)

When I look at the scar on my left arm, I still consider this a disgraceful, violent act—an older boy stabbing a little lad just to show the gang how big he was.

This whole area was full of violence and theft and I remember people talking about such-and-such being raped. I didn't know what that meant at the time, so it didn't mean much to me.

Over the many days and nights of the blitz of 1940/41, South West London, and, more particularly, Battersea, was targeted by the Luftwaffe. It was probable that the German air force were trying to destroy the Battersea Power Station.

The iconic four-chimney structure still sits on the south bank of the River Thames. It remains one of the world's largest brick structures and is a Grade II listed building, and yet, somehow, the Luftwaffe missed it when they dropped their bombs.

Sadly, my Auntie Rose, Uncle Jack, and their little dog, were killed in one of those night bombings when their house took a direct hit.

Auntie Rose was one of the ladies who had stood crying and wiping their eyes the day I left home as an evacuee. She had hugged and kissed me and wished me well as I began my journey into the countryside to see the ducks. I don't remember her or her husband, Uncle Jack, but their images have since been pointed out to me in the family photo album.

Some years after the war ended, I heard my parents discussing my Auntie's jewellery. Mum's eyes brimmed with tears as she recalled the shock of having to go to a makeshift mortuary in Battersea to identify her sister and brother-in-law's bodies. Though they had been subject to an explosion, she was able to recognise them. Mum's distress was intensified, when she noticed two of her sister's fingers had been cut off below the knuckles and the rings she wore on those fingers had been stolen.

I had still been a young lad when I overheard this conversation but repeated it to several people to find out if this was an unusual crime. To my disgust, I learned that this was commonplace. Thieves, carrying clippers in their pockets, rushed to bombed out sites where houses had been destroyed and the bodies needed to be removed. This had to be carried out with haste and the public kept away. There could be unseen dangers such as unexploded bombs, gas leakages, severed electrical cables, and there was, of course, the horror of finding bodies blown to pieces. The clean-up and rescue teams picked their way through piles of rubble which hours before had been happy family homes where mothers cooked meals and tucked their children up in bed. Now tiles fell from roofs hanging precariously over pathways and the dead and dying lay buried under broken bricks, rafters, and grey plaster dust which covered everything—whole families were obliterated in seconds.

War, in every aspect, is disgraceful, but there is no baser act than to mutilate and rob from a corpse for personal gain. That person was someone's loved one. It appears that some men had no conscience and so the practice of using clippers on dead victims became a common occurrence.

Untold carnage took place every day and night and unskilled labourers were hired to dig through the streets of destroyed houses and piles of rubble searching for survivors and the dead. The blitz was heaviest in London and Coventry and men arrived from various areas outside England to volunteer to carry out this unpleasant job. I will not say where they came from as I have great respect for their country and the majority of men who came, but what kind of person would volunteer to do this awful work day after day?

I have wanted, for a moment, to stray from my personal story into the fringe of war to give this lesser known account—but there is still much more I will never tell.

The misery in the area was compounded by the grey put put planes flying overhead and dropping death down on everyone.

My time here was thankfully cut short when an idiot in a black coat appeared at the front door carrying a bag of papers. Another move was imminent. Now my name had been changed and I didn't understand why. I was also informed that my family were not in England.

The idiot asked, "Do you speak any other languages?"

I obliged by counting from one to ten in German.

A lady took me to a large wooden shed somewhere in London where another idiot rattled off something I didn't understand. I was taken to an administration centre and then a long journey commenced. I'd obviously been mixed up with someone else. This change of name would have made it very difficult for Mrs Plumbridge to trace me.

I don't think the mix-up was intentional. Most of the men were still at war so the understaffed authorities consisted of women and older men, most of whom were inexperienced in such matters. Their main concern was survival—making sure they didn't fall victim to bombs and doodle bug attacks.

An official from the ministry had heard me speak to the German Prisoners of War in their native tongue when I was swinging on the garden gate. He'd walked across the road and asked me if I were German. I told him 'no' and he left. It's possible that this contributed to the mix up.

How wonderful this war was for me? What had happened to the ducks I'd set off to see all those years ago? Maybe they didn't like the war and flew away.

(2) Over ten thousand V1s were launched towards Britain during World War Two flying at speeds of four hundred miles per hour and at altitudes of up to three thousand feet. Men, woman, and children would hear this mindless rocket becoming louder and louder as it flew nearer to them. Then the engine would stop and the V1 would drop out of the sky. As long as you could hear the engine you were all right, but if the engine stopped, you knew it was coming down and would wreak devastation and death somewhere near you, or, even worse, you might be killed.

Chapter 9

A Long Journey

I was again fitted out with a brown label holding my new name and other information and was told to look after it.

This time I wasn't given a cardboard box to hang around my neck. By now, the authorities had realised the enemy were not going to use gas warfare on the United Kingdom, so gas masks were no long being issued.

I boarded a train and stared out of the window at the passing hedges, trees, fields, and the occasional houses dotted around the countryside. It was a long journey and I eventually arrived with a hundred other children at a railway station where we disembarked, walked across the platform, and climbed a flight of stairs. A large sign read 'Bolton'. I was in Lancashire. Everything looked dark and dirty.

We assembled in two long rows, girls in one and boys in the other, and marched up the road. Within five minutes I hated the place. Everything was built of dark stone. The roads and streets were cobbled, and people wore funny boots called clogs.

(Working men's shoes were made of leather cowhide with buckle clasps over wooden soles shod with iron. They kept the feet dry in rain or snow.)

This place was a total shock to me. It was so different from Bedfordshire and Middlesex although it did resemble parts of London. We walked past a huge mill chimney. Its size and foreboding appearance terrified me. I'd never seen a mill.

I could do nothing but follow the line of children who seemed, like me, to be in shock at where we had arrived after our arduous train journey. I could see my breath and everything looked damp. I hated everything about it.

It would be unheard of today for hundreds of unaccompanied children to journey two hundred miles with no parents into an environment where they had no support and no arranged accommodation. Yet this happened at the bequest of some idiots sitting at their desks in London. Many of the boys and girls, were tiny and scared. How could this happen?!

You may reason that as we were at war, the authorities had to send children to a safe place, but Bolton was not a safe place; the ruins of bombed out homes and offices lay around us. Liverpool and its docks were the main targets for German bombers, but some dropped their bombs on Bolton on their way back to Germany. We had been transported all the way from London into this environment. Unbelievable.

I had lived in many homes and hostels around the United Kingdom but had never felt so alone and lost as I did now. As I walked with the other children towards the place we would call home for the next few days, I had no idea what was in store for me. I was not a lucky lad and for reasons unknown I had to use that new name.

We arrived at a church school and were taken into a make-shift dormitory and told to stand next to our low canvas beds. A lady came along and gave us a bag of biscuits, a small pillow, and two blankets.

A man appeared, quieted us down, and told us someone would pick us up when the public came in, but before this we had to look our best. Anyone with glasses had to put them in their pocket.

He told us, "Pull up your socks, boys, do up your flies, and everyone wash your face and hands." Another lady went from child to child putting a brush through our hair—the same brush for everyone. "Answer any questions with 'yes, Sir' or 'no, Sir'" he continued, "and make sure your noses are wiped."

The bell rang, and we stood at the end of our canvas beds and in came the people to inspect the scruffy mob who had arrived that day from all over the south. It was like a cattle market. I think all the girls went first then some boys. I didn't get chosen so spent the night on my canvas bed.

The next day those who hadn't been selected by families were moved round and advised to smile at everyone. A lady appeared with her daughter and asked me my name. I told her and finished with 'madam'. She picked me and off we went to a nice house opposite a park called Green Lane. I'd no luggage, only the clothes I was wearing. She was a pleasant lady with a friendly daughter though I couldn't understand a word she spoke. I still hated Bolton, but at least I'd a nice person, a home, and a bed.

The food was excellent. I spent most of my time in the small park opposite the house, but soon the WVS lady arrived. She told me the lady I was staying with had cut off her hand in a machine at work and was in hospital. I was moving again.

The WVS lady took me to Bolton Police Station in the town centre where I slept in a cell with bars on the front and a large sliding opening. There was no home readily available for me so this would be my home until they found one.

I enjoyed the food, and the policemen were kind and showed me all around the station.

One of them took me to Bolton Civic Centre near the Town Hall steps where a large tent had been erected. A lady inspected my brown label and told me to step inside. This Canadian Refugee Tent contained a wonderland of American and Canadian clothing.

I had to stand still and be fitted out with trousers, socks, shorts, shirt, and a jumper and overcoat but no vest or underpants. Still wearing my old clothes, I went with the police officer back to my cell and then to the bath area. After being cleaned up, I was allowed to put on my Canadian clothes. How different I looked! I began to feel a little more favourable towards Bolton.

A policeman told me that being outfitted in the new clothes would help to move me on to another home, which is what happened. Viewers came to the Police Station, and I was picked by a family who took me by tram to an area of Bolton called Daubhill. Once home, the parents showed me to my room at the back of the small house.

A cobbled back yard led to the WC known as a tippler toilet. Often these were shared by two, three, or even four households. Tippler toilets didn't have a flushing system so waste remained in an open sewer until the tippler filled with the waste kitchen sink water. It would then tip, sending a couple of gallons of water through the system and flushing the waste away. This created a bad odour in warm weather, but at least it was not too near the house.

The new family had a lad who was older than me by two or three years. They had wanted to get a friend for him, but this didn't work out as I didn't want any friends especially someone I couldn't understand. They enrolled me at Emmanuel Church School, but I found this not to my liking. Firstly, I couldn't understand the teacher, and, secondly, nobody wanted to get involved with the 'evacuee with a brown label'.

One lad, a boy of colour, was also a refugee. He'd come from Jersey, which was occupied by the Germans. His short, black, curly hair fascinated me. We became friends at once. He was older than me by two years but had a friendly nature and was always smiling. I had to listen hard to understand him and I couldn't pronounce his name, so I called him Jersey.

Every morning, he came to the little terraced house where I lived, and, for protection and companionship, we walked to school and back home together.

The local tough boys didn't like refugees—the other, more popular name for evacuees. They would gang up and wait for me after school, working together to trap me in a back street. I was forced to fight the biggest one of the mob while the others stood around me in a ring. So, if there were two of us standing back to back and moving around in a circle, we were more difficult to hit and we stood a chance. With Jersey at my back I felt safe.

Many years after our introduction to Bolton life, the Asian boys got the same treatment until there were enough of them to gang up and look after themselves.

My new home was near the large park which spread out on both sides of Quebec Street. I noticed the street gang of cowards ran off to the swings and slides after our fights together.

Nearby, was a rope manufacturer. This was to prove to my advantage. I waited until the time was right and no one was around, then took two handfuls of tallow, (a yellow grease for the ropes) from the barrels near the factory door. I ran back to the park and walked up the slide the wrong way around and smeared tallow all over it. The results were as hoped: tallow grease up the bullies legs and back.

I wasn't happy living with the new family; their attitude towards me changed and there was no pleasure in the house. They told me 'do this', 'why did you not do that', or 'go there', 'get that', 'clean this', 'move that', 'don't sit there', 'go out for an hour', 'where have you been?' 'did you get that?'

Once or twice a week, the son and I were made to have boxing matches in the front room. I didn't have a choice in this.

The gloves they made me wear were too big. The other lad looked down at me and smirked. He was two years older, so it was an unfair fight to begin with, and the father always urged him on: 'hit him there or there', 'use your left or right'. No one ever shouted for me, and when I did get a good punch in the fight was stopped. I was a human punchbag. I disliked Bolton and the people who lived there, and I still couldn't understand their accent.

Jersey and I decided to make some money. He'd a good knowledge of the mouth-organ and he also showed me what he called 'bones'—two pieces about six inches long which he put between his fingers and clapped up and down, clickety click.

He showed me what to do. It took me hours of practice to get the rhythm correct. Next, he showed me how to clap my hands over the bones, which changed the sound.

After many hours of practice, we perfected three marching tunes. One, called 'Georgia', was an American marching song from their Civil War, and another was called 'Yankee Doodle Dandy'.

We went to pubs, cinema queues, theatre queues, and fish and chip shops with our three marching tunes, mouth organ, and bones. After performing, we went down the queues asking for something for the refugees' collection.

Theatre queues were the best and there seemed to be theatres all over Bolton. We increased our repertoire from three tunes to five with a little singing thrown in, and on a good Friday or Saturday night we would make around five shillings split two ways.

The big day came when a well-dressed man stood watching us perform outside the Grand Theatre and told us to step inside. He asked us to go on stage and play a few tunes to the audience while the curtain was down. We agreed and he walked onto the stage and told the people that two refugees would entertain them for a few minutes.

With a wide sweep of his hand he said, "Ladies and gentlemen, I give you 'The Jersey Boys'."

Not only did we play the marching tunes, we also marched up and down the stage and finished our last tune marching off into the wings. The audience clapped and shouted 'more'.

Jersey and I looked at each other wide-eyed. We were thrilled and began to cry as the emotion took over us. We had both been kicked around all our lives and now people were applauding our efforts on the stage, how wonderful!

The well-dressed man, who we found out was the manager, took us by the hand and led us, back onto the stage to more applause. I sniffed and wiped my eyes with the back of my hand and looked out at the crowd.

He asked us if we could come back the following Saturday evening and gave us ten shillings. From there we went to the U.C.P Shop for a hot, sit-down dinner with mashed potato and a mug of tea.

Point of fact: United Cattle Products (U.C.P.) Ltd. was a chain of shops and restaurants in the North of England which specialised in tripe dishes, and provided ox tail, cow heel, and other bovine extremities in an age when little was wasted.

Our lives changed overnight. I suddenly liked Bolton. When we added up our week's earnings, we had nearly three pounds to add to the theatre manager's ten shillings. Jersey and I decided there and then we were no longer interested in going to school. We were fed up with the constant violence and had something now that was our own.

We kept the name 'The Jersey Boys' and went to Harker & Howarths, the musical shop. I wanted to learn to play an instrument. It had to be something I could carry around so it couldn't be too big.

We told the man in the shop we were The Jersey Boys and had played on stage at The Grand. Eventually, we found a recorder which suited me, but I had to start from scratch. The shopkeeper showed me where to put my fingers and told me to put my thumb over the hole at the back. He instructed me to tip the hole at the back to go higher up the scale.

The noise I produced was enough to frighten the deaf, but as I'd stopped going to school, there was plenty of time in which to practice. To keep things right at home, Jersey came around in the morning every day as usual, but we had to find somewhere warm to go during school-time. I had an idea.

I took Jersey to the town centre Police Station to meet my policeman friends and get a cup of hot cocoa. Two of the policemen remembered me, so I asked them if they knew of a warm place where we could practice our music as we were on at The Grand. The Jersey Boys would soon be the top act. They took us to a building near the Town Hall where a lady gave us a cup of tea and a slice of cake. There were lots of vacant rooms because many of the staff had been moved to another building away from the town centre for protection against air-raids.

I think the lady expected light entertainment from The Jersey Boys but instead got a sound from the recorder akin to a cat being tortured. While we were in the town centre we called in at the Canadian Refugee Tent for more clothes. I was already registered, so we registered Jersey and he got rigged out from head to toe. Bolton was looking a little better every day.

Jersey asked his father to play with us. I didn't know he played an instrument and was stunned when I heard him playing the banjo. He could really play. He told me his style was New Orleans. His fingers seemed to pluck the strings, but once he got going and Jersey came in with the mouth organ and I joined in on the bones, it was magic. We became The Three Jersey Boys. His father drove us along with his plucking style on the Banjo, continually changing chords and rhythm. What a fabulous sound we made. After a few rehearsals we were ready for an audience, but not the cinema queues or public houses, we were above that now.

Jersey's dad decided to try two other theatres in Bolton and arranged for us to play for the staff and cleaners. They loved us and recommended us to the managers, and we did a full rehearsal. No-one in Bolton had ever heard of New Orleans music; this was way ahead of its time there. It had what people called 'jump'. (So, The Jersey Boys had jump.)

We performed again at The Grand Theatre with great success. People loved our sound and shouted 'more' as we left the stage. We also performed at the Majestic Theatre on St. Helens Road. The latter is long gone. Majestics Van Hire stands on the site nowadays, named after the old theatre run by Mr G Sinnot and his wife Adel. We also performed at the Labour Club on Wigan Road and many other places whose names I can't remember.

When I first came to stay with this family, I slept under the stairs with the dog, but now I was out at night so much they provided me with a blanket and told me to sleep in the outside toilet.

I also obtained a large army coat which I kept hidden. When I arrived at the rear gate late at night, on went the army coat (which was at least ten sizes too big). I'd go inside and shut the toilet door, sit on the toilet with my legs up against the middle bar of wood which ran horizontally across the inside of the door, and wrap everything round me, my blanket folded up to make a pillow. This was fabulous as long as I was sitting well down the toilet. If I wedged myself in place, I was nice and warm and fast asleep in no time.

Chapter 10

Another Move

At six every morning I had to step out of the toilet shed because the man of the house with whom I was living wanted to use it before going to work. When he'd left, I could go back in and snooze away till around 8:30am.

I'd then hide my coat and blanket, walk to a public washhouse in Bolton town centre, and wash in hot water with soap—for the cost of a penny. Afterwards I'd cross the road and wander into the U.C.P. Shop in Bradshaw Gate and tuck into a half breakfast: small tea, mash, peas, and sausage with brown sauce and a slice of bread, all for sixpence. That was a great start to the day. afterwards, I'd meet Jersey at our rehearsal room in the Town Hall annex. The nice lady who made tea for the staff would sometimes give me a large cup of tea and a slice of toast.

Two things brought me to yet another move. The first was that one night whilst asleep in my toilet, what I presumed was a cat slipped under the door and climbed onto my warm lap for a sleep. I stroked it and it settled down. There was no street lighting in wartime Britain. Because of the likelihood of air raids, the street lamps were not lit and people had to use thick, blackout curtains in their windows. This made it harder for the enemy aircraft to find their targets, but it also made it impossible to see the animal sleeping on my lap. After a while I noticed it had a thin tail. This wasn't a cat, it was a big, fat sewer-rat. I might have gasped or said something, because it jumped off my lap and ran back under the door. Now I couldn't get back to sleep.

The second reason for my move was Tom, whom I met near my 'residence'. Tom was an ex-miner who had developed a lung disease from inhaling coal dust whilst working down the mines. He never stopped coughing, so I called him 'Tom the Cougher' or 'Coughing Tom'.

He rented a small lockup yard where he made just enough coal bricks for him and a friend. I often sat with him around the fire he'd made with wood and coal-bricks, listening to his mining stories, and keeping warm. When, in passing, I told him about the rat sleeping on my lap, he became angry and asked me to go around the corner to his house and meet his sister, Janet. Neither had got married, so they lived together. I felt at home with Coughing Tom and got on well with him and his sister.

When Tom described my sleeping arrangements to Janet and told her of my furry night visitor, she didn't hesitate in saying I should move in with them. I agreed, and she showed me my small bedroom. I couldn't wait to snuggle under the clean sheets and feel the rug under my bare feet when I got up in the mornings. After wedging myself in an outside toilet for months, it would be wonderful to stretch out at night and sleep in a comfortable bed... and it would be much more hygienic too.

Tom and Janet had an inside toilet and hot water from a back boiler, what luxury.

I returned to my so-called home and informed the family I was moving out. They didn't want me there and were only interested in the fifteen shillings a week they received from the government for my keep. They handed me my ration book and said 'goodbye for now'. It was as simple as that. There was no argument, and no one tried to convince me to stay. I collected my army coat and walked away.

I arrived back at coughing Tom's with a huge grin on my face and agreed to go to the High Street Baths every Saturday for a bath and to wash my hair.

After paying the required three-pence admittance fee to the baths, which included payment for soap, and the use of a towel, I walked into a wet room, stripped off, and sat in one of the several blue-grey stone troughs which were set out in rows. Each man sat in his own trough. Hot water ran in at one end of the trough and washed across where you were sitting and ran out of the other end and into the next trough, and so on. This same water ran in a single circuit through the troughs one after another before pouring down the drain.

This created a problem. You started off at the trough furthest from the water supply, so when the water reached you it had been through all the other troughs, and, as most of the men there were miners who had been working the night shift down the pit, it was black.

As the men finished washing, I made my way down the troughs until I got to the clean water, then I picked up the soap they had left and had a good wash. This process took about an hour. The miners got to know me and nicknamed me 'Little Cock' (I wonder why). These were hard but good men and they took to the little lad who appeared every Saturday.

After a time, if the miners were still outside the baths when I came out, one would pick me up, carry me under his arm, and off we would go to the pubs down Derby Street. The beer was Magee-Marshal which came from a brewery on the same road, and Halcroft Ales who also had a brewery in Bolton.

(Many years afterwards I purchased their land and eight houses in Bolton, but that is another story).

The miners took me to the pubs with them, which was not allowed, but they didn't care; I was their little mascot. They gave me a glass of lemonade and sometimes a black pudding and bread, or a meat pie, and potato and pig's trotters. I felt safe with these wonderful men. They moved from pub to pub drinking at each, but after two or three pubs I used to leave. The tram ran up Derby Street and I could ride for nothing because I was an evacuee. I'd return home and meet them again at the High Street Baths the following Saturday.

Bolton didn't appeal to me any more now than it had when I first set my eyes on its dark, stoney streets, but certain people were making my life much more enjoyable: the miners, Coughing Tom and Janet, Jersey and his dad, the lady in the Town Hall annex who looked after me with tea and toast, the ladies in the U.C.P. who always gave me more than I paid for, the attendant at the baths, the attendant at my wash rooms in St Peter's Square. These were good, decent people who seemed interested in helping the little evacuee lad with the funny accent.

Chapter 11

Only Three-pence a brick

I watched Coughing Tom fill a bucket from the slag heaped on the yard floor. He mixed it with some small coal chips and tipped the mixture into a wooden brick mould. Rectangular and clearly heavy, the sides were a little higher than an imperial-sized brick sitting flat on its bottom. Inside the frame, vertical and horizontal dividers separated the mould into nine equally sized, rectangular spaces. Once Tom was satisfied the slag was evenly distributed, he placed the heavy wooden lid on top and compacted the mix using a press bar. The slag had been a little moist, so the water dripped out of the bottom.

"Is that it? Are the bricks made now?" I asked, eager faced.

Coughing Tom smiled. "No. We leave them twenty-four hours. Tomorrow, I'll get them out of the frame and heat them on the coke stove. That'll harden them."

The following day Tom dismantled the press and tipped the hardened coal bricks out. One broke into two pieces.

He explained, "That'll burn just as well." I looked at the coal dust which had fallen between the bricks. "The dust won't go to waste either," he added. "You sprinkle it over the fire, and it forms a seal and will keep the house warm all night." He paused and stood upright. "The more coal dust I have, the more bricks I can make and sell."

Right now, this was only a hobby, but I was very interested and could see a potential business opportunity.

I told Jersey about it. We needed transport, so Jersey and I walked across the road to Coughing Tom's yard in Quebeck Street. Under the rain cover was a stack of items various people had asked him to mind for them over the months and years. Some had never returned to collect their belongings. I sorted through these things and found a large pram with big wheels and springs.

Jersey and I pushed it down Manchester Road near to the football ground and to the large man-made slag heap. The slag heap had become a landmark to regulars. They were used to seeing it, but a stranger might find the enormity of its black, ominous appearance quite foreboding.

We filled the pram with slag and between us pushed the heavy load all the way up Derby Street to Coughing Tom's premises. He was delighted. Now he could make more bricks. We wheeled the pram to the slag heap and filled it three times a day. This gave us about three dozen bricks.

Jersey and I sold these at fish and chip shops, pubs, and local houses. Each day we pushed and pulled the pram full of bricks along the streets. It was heavy and this was hard work, and beads of sweat soon joined the coal dust on our faces. Before long we were as black as the coal-bricks, and Jersey's teeth looked even whiter than usual.

One day the bottom fell out of the pram depositing coal dust all over the road. We couldn't get it back in the pram, so Jersey stood guard over it while I went off to get some potato sacks. I returned to a grinning Jersey and no slag spill. He was clearly pleased with himself. The people had appeared out of the houses carrying buckets and Jersey had sold most of the dust to them.

"I charged three pennies a bucket," he said.

Coal dust was used a lot. It was excellent at keeping fires burning slowly throughout the night, until around 6 am when the people awoke to start their long, hard day's work in the noisy mills and factories.

While Tom repaired the pram, we continued with our services using an old, abandoned wooden pram.

We priced our bricks at three-pence apiece or a penny-ha'penny for a broken half, thus, for a shilling, the customers had four bricks which would last them four evenings. We could only carry twelve bricks in our pram as they were heavy, but we sold them all in an hour and earned three shillings—a good amount of money for free coal dust.

We repeated this three or four times a day, and, if we could have kept up with demand, could have doubled our market. We had to figure out a way of producing more coal-bricks.

While we were around the town, Jersey and I noticed many people getting on the trams with suit cases and large bags. This could be the answer; we could use the tram system. Jersey and I spoke to the conductors. I can't remember the financial arrangements, but, as long as we kept the trams clean, they agreed to let us go ahead.

We transported four bags of dust on the tram at a time which gave us twenty-six bricks. Doing this twice a day gave us enough dust for approximately fifty bricks. This, in turn, earned us one pound ten shillings a day totalling nine pounds per week on a six-day week.

This was a good start to our business, but, again, we knew we could sell three times that amount of bricks, and half the time Coughing Tom had to sit waiting for the next delivery of coal dust. There had to be a way of increasing output.

We thought up various methods, and, as we were talking, a gypsy man with a pony and flat trailer stopped and asked us if we had any soap.

At once, I saw our chance to increase the coal dust supply. I asked the man if he was interested in collecting our coal dust and how much he'd charge. We worked out a system which suited us all and so we gave him his first job.

We went with him to the slag heap and loaded up ten sacks—he helped which saved time—then clip clop up Derby Street, and the job was done: ten sacks of dust. Coughing Tom told us to bring two loads a day. The gypsy man agreed, and we paid him five pounds per week for his short trips up and down Derby Street. We had enough dust in each load to make fifty bricks so that made us one hundred bricks per day. Between us, we now made eighteen pounds per week. This was excellent; in those days the average employee's wage was six pounds per week.

However, we were organised for only a short time because our gypsy man sometimes didn't turn up.

One morning, he came to our premises and said, "I'm moving away. Do you want to buy the pony and rig?"

We asked him to come back the following day. The purchase would save us five pounds a week, but the horse would need stabling with fresh water.

Coughing Tom told us there was a stable at the rear of the yard which was warm and dry and had running water to keep the place clean. Now all we needed was a supply of fresh straw. This wouldn't be a problem. A couple of people on Bolton Market sold straw at a reasonable price. Now we wondered how much the man would want for his horse and rig.

The next day, he arrived at the yard and unhitched the strong, black and white horse from the rig. We asked him about his price.

He looked towards us and said, "A handful."

Tom smiled. "What's a handful?"

"Twenty quid."

Coughing Tom, Jersey, and I looked at each other, shocked at such a low price. Tom walked over and inspected the horse. "The blacksmith will need to work on him, but I know a local one." He walked around the rig. "This needs work too. I can do that."

We paid the man, and he left. Tom's blacksmith always heard all the latest news from the various gypsy camps. When we took the horse to him, he told us our gypsy friend had sold the horse and rig so cheaply because he owed money to a group of gypsies from another camp. They were pursuing him and his rig and he needed the money to get away.

Our man had gone into hiding with the twenty pounds, but we now had a good, four-year-old horse and a decent flat rig. Jersey and I only had to pay Coughing Tom what he'd outlaid for the blacksmith and repairs and we would be even and ready to continue our business.

Chapter 12

Home from Home

Jersey ate his food with us and moved into the stable to guard the horse at night—just in case the gypsies tried to steal it. I didn't go to the High Street Baths anymore. Instead, Janet bathed me in a galvanised tin bath she kept hanging on the rear wall of the house.

On bath nights, she brought it into the living room, poured warm water into it, and placed a house brick under one end to make it deeper at the other. I still remember the smell of the green, carbolic soap she used to give me and Jersey a good scrub in front of the roaring fire, sometimes whilst we ate bread and jam.

We soon got the hang of the rig and horse, and feeding, brushing, and mucking him out. Our business thrived and now we sold horse manure and straw to the people at the big houses for their homegrown strawberries.

We had a horse vet look over our investment. We were in luck; the animal was in excellent condition, but the vet advised us to put a blanket over him at night even though he slept on straw. I called the horse, Peter, after my beloved Suffolk Punch in Buckinghamshire.

Coughing Tom seemed to cough less and thrived on making coal-bricks. Jack, an ex-miner friend of his turned up to help him. He also had a persistent cough, so we called them 'The Coughing Twins'.

We expanded our market and now made around a thousand bricks per week. The new bricks were larger than the original ones, so we sold them at fourpence per brick and tuppence per broken half. This earned us forty pounds a week.

Jersey and I had five pounds each, the horse cost us five pounds per week for food, straw, and vet bills, and Coughing Tom had ten pounds. I lived free of charge, but Janet held my ration book and had the money from the Government for housing an evacuee. After paying five shillings rent for the house (in today's money twenty-five pence per week), and four shillings per week for the stable (twenty pence today), we put aside about twelve pounds per week for any overheads. This belonged to us all.

We soon found another way to make money. When we called to their houses to deliver bricks, many people asked us if we could deliver their bets on horses to a bookmaker. (Gambling was illegal unless the bookie had a license).

On our journeys around Bolton we noticed the whereabouts of an illegal bookmaker. We called into his office and asked if he wanted us to collect his bets. After he'd checked we were honest and dependable, he agreed and said he'd pay us ten percent commission on any turnover we brought to him.

Soon, when several people paid us for their bricks, they gave us their bets, which we took to the bookmaker. We soon figured out another earner; sometimes we stood the bets ourselves. We gave the bookmaker seven out of every ten bets we received and kept what Tom called the 'silly bets'. Whatever we made on the betting side was kept separate from the brick money.

We then printed a sign in black and white along the side of the rig which read 'FOR HIRE WITH HORSE AND DRIVER'. People stopped us and asked if we did furniture removal. We said we did, but it was their responsibility to load, tie up, and secure their goods, and to go with us to the delivery destination to unload the furniture. We demanded payment before the furniture was unloaded.

Bolton Fruit Market gave us work making deliveries around the town, which meant we had plenty of carrots and cabbage for our horse, and fresh fruit, potatoes, and vegetables for ourselves. I was liking Bolton a little more each day.

Our landlord, who also owned the stables we worked from, approached us one day. He told us both properties were in a family trust, and, as his mother had died, all the property they owned had to be sold. As a sitting tenant, he gave Coughing Tom first option to buy both properties for seventy-five pounds.

We held a family meeting to discuss this with Coughing Tom in charge. We scraped together forty-two pounds and arranged another meeting with the landlord. He accepted the initial payment of the forty-two pounds with the proviso we paid the remaining thirty-three pounds, with interest, over a twelve-month period. Coughing Tom and Janet would own everything. At around eight years old, I was too young to have property put in my name anyway.

Jersey and I had lived with Coughing Tom and Janet for about a year and she never charged us for food or board, so we were delighted to help this wonderful couple. We now had a good business, a house, and a yard, a stable, and our own transport with a young, fit horse... how we had progressed from lugging coal slag in an old pram and producing a dozen bricks per week.

Chapter 13

The Fight

After delivering bricks, picking up betting slips and money, dropping off market vegetables at the shops, selling bags of manure and whatever else we did, Jersey and I called back to see Coughing Tom at the yard.

A few men were there giving him a hard time. When we appeared, a lad who was with them, ran over to us and snatched the reins of our horse.

"This is it," he said looking at the others. "It's ours."

I jumped off the rig and pushed him away. He took a swing at me and struck me in the face. I fell down but got back up and thumped him in the eye and kicked him. This lad was taller than me, strong and meaty, a bully boy, red-faced and full of fight.

A burly man parted us. "A fight has to be done on Saturday, with proper rules as to the gypsy law."

I didn't know what he meant, but it was arranged. I had to be at Quebec Street fields near the slide and swings at 1pm the following Saturday. The men left.

Tom informed us the gypsy from whom we had purchased the horse and rig owed these men money and they had come to seize the rig as payment. We had no contracted receipt to prove we had paid for the rig so what were we to do now?

After discussion, we decided to let things die down and leave it be. This fight was the next issue. Tom said I couldn't fight that gypsy lad because he at least two years older and was too big and strong for me. I didn't give it much thought. I was more worried about our horse and rig and the risk of it disappearing. For the next few nights, Jersey and I slept with the horse in the yard.

Saturday soon came around and my young friend and I went off to collect coal dust, then to Bolton Market to pick up sacks of potatoes, before returning to the yard. Jersey reminded me of the meeting I had at 1 pm on the Quebec Street playing fields.

It was not far short of 1pm, so we walked down to the field along Walter Street. Our mouths dropped open and we looked at each other with wide open eyes. There were horses and traps everywhere. It looked like a gypsy holiday gathering or special event. Everyone had turned out to see our fight. My stomach turned over and I became short of breath; I think they call it fear.

We walked onto the playing fields. The gypsy boys surrounded us and assumed it was Jersey who was fighting and not me. I told them I was fighting, and Jersey was my second. I had the fastest beating heart in Bolton. What had I got into with this mob? A big man appeared.

He pushed the people back and laughed when he saw me. "Are you fighting today?"

"Yes, I'm ready."

At the man's directive, the large crowd moved back forming a circle. I spotted three or four miners who I knew and waved to them. I wanted them near me for support. They stepped across the circle and came over to me asking what I was doing there. I told them I was fighting and asked them to look after me if I got hurt.

"Remove your clogs and always move to the right away from his right," one of them told me, trying to even out the fight a little.

I didn't know my right from left so that was no help. They showed me with a movement, and I got the message. They looked at the big gypsy lad.

Another told me, "Keep away from him, hit him, and move away. Keep on the move. That's right. Take your clogs off. They'll stick to the grass.

The big man called us together in the middle of the ring and told us the rules: no kicking when down on the grass, no fingers in eyes, if you turn your back the fight's over, and when I shout you part and go to the edge of the grass circle."

While I was listening, a tremendous thump to my left ear knocked me to the ground. The gypsy lad had overstepped the mark. The big man pulled him to one side and hit him around the face.

I was giddy from the blow so was allowed time to recover, but things soon got going. I danced in and out and hit the older boy in the face several times. He rushed at me swinging punches. One or two hit me but not full on. His nose bled down his chin and the blood marked his shirt. I aimed at his face with every blow. His body was big and hard; striking that would be pointless.

He hit my ribs with full force, and I went down on the grass but got up and laid into him. My hands hurt, my knuckles were skinned where I'd hit his teeth, and there was something wrong with my thumbs.

Adrenalin rushed through my body. All fear was gone. I'd taken many punches but had hit him with several good blows to the head.

Blood ran down his face from a cut next to his eye and his lips were fat and cut. He spat out blood. He'd got a few good blows in near my eyes too, but the damage was superficial.

The big man stood between us and asked if we wanted to carry on the fight. I nodded and so did my opponent. I went back to my side of the circle and the miners surrounded me. One bent his leg and I sat on it like a chair. Weeks of lifting and hauling bricks had stood me in good stead; I was only slightly out of breath.

Because I'd never been shown the correct way to punch, my thumbs had been pushed back into my hands. One of the men straightened them out and showed me the correct way to make a fist and turn my hand inwards. He also spat on my hands.

The big gypsy man walked to the centre of the muddy circle and waved us to resume, which we did. The big lad tried a new tactic. He started rushing in at me kicking. Because I had no clogs on, I could move away quickly and dodge him. His leg came up. I grabbed it and pulled his foot up in the air. He fell to the ground. I kept hold of his foot and pulled his leg right back over his body. He shouted out in pain then got up and hopped around on one leg. He'd seen a different side to me at last. He stopped rushing about and swinging but still held his fists up ready to fight. I darted in and punched him on the nose and jaw, then he struck me a very hard blow to my ribs. I heard a snapping noise and red-hot pain shot through my chest. I couldn't breathe.

The boy took hold of my head and hit me with his forehead. I went giddy again and blood rushed down my nose. I remember getting a grip on his arm and biting his hand at the same time. I forced my knee into his groin, and he fell onto his knees holding his crotch. I followed through with a knee under his jaw, twice. His front teeth sank into my leg. Through hazy vision I glanced down at the bloody wound where the lad's front teeth were still imbedded. The big gypsy man came between us and lifted me up to his chest.

When I opened my eyes, I was lying on a small bed in his caravan. There was no winner. We had both fought well and each had inflicted terrible damage on the other. The gypsy boy and I later became friends.

***

Through life's many up's and down's, my friendship with the gypsy people still stands out as being very special to me. After a spell in the local cottage hospital, I stayed with them and they looked after me as I recuperated.

But this was only one aspect of their friendship. Over a period of time, I learned from their conversations that they wanted me to live with them and were willing to accept me as one of their own.

The gypsy ladies surrounded me with love and sincerity. The men were hard but sincere, and every week I turned up with our horse and nosebag and ate with them.

I never returned home without food and clothing. On occasions I stayed in a caravan overnight and was given an enormous breakfast in the morning. My horse was washed and brushed and his nosebag filled with fresh grain.

When the gypsies held get-togethers, I was collected from Tom's yard and travelled with them, clip clopping, to a farm where there would be food and gypsy dancing. Gallons of beer and cider was drunk, and fires were lit, and all manner of meat cooked with homemade bread and home-grown vegetables and fruits.

I think I was around nine years old at this time. The men introduced me to various gypsy girls and invited me to choose one before they were spoken for. It was a little awkward as I knew nothing about girls and wasn't really interested, which made things worse. But this soon passed and there were plenty of young gypsy boys to befriend.

I learned a little later that if you choose a young gypsy girl and a young gypsy boy wants her too, you have to fight for her, so, I'm glad I didn't get involved.

***

Now back to the fight...

I couldn't move, every part of me ached, my eye wouldn't open, my hands were swollen and stiff, my thumbs wouldn't work, whenever I moved or took a deep breath a terrible pain shot through my chest, my mouth hurt, and I'd lost one of my teeth. I'd been very badly beaten and there were blue marks all over my body. The joints of both thumbs had to be pulled out and repositioned because the bones were out of joint and had gone inwards, I'd a broken finger, my top lip was split open, and I couldn't hear with my left ear. (My hearing was permanently damaged, and I still have the scar on my leg where the gypsy boy's teeth embedded in it.) I went into the fight as a small boy and came out with tenacity and the knowledge that I could overcome anything life was to throw at me. I would never run away from anything.

The big gypsy man (whose name, I learned, was Sol), and his wife looked after me. She was a beautiful, olive skinned woman with dark hair and deep brown eyes. She placed warm cloths on my arms, chest, and shoulders. The next thing I remember was being in hospital with a tight wrapping round my chest—one of my ribs was broken. I slept for two days and then Sol took me back to his home in the caravan. His wife was wonderful. I was given soup and she covered me in some kind of oil and rubbed my hands, shoulders, and neck. I kept falling asleep; my body was exhausted, and I had no strength. I was told later that Jersey and Coughing Tom came 'round every day.

There was no further trouble from the gypsy boys. Peter the horse and the rig were ours and the fight on the grass was the talk of the camp. After around two weeks, I was allowed to sit outside next to the caravan in the sunshine with the family's three dogs. After another week I received a visit from three gypsy boys, all of whom wanted to be my friend. The lady looking after me had told other gypsies she wanted me to stay with them since I had no family, so I asked if I was staying for good. I was half-convinced it would be a good thing for me to live with the gypsy family; everybody seemed to like me, I had visitors every day, and most gypsy ladies gave me food or an item of homemade clothing.

The miners at the fight had told the other gypsy boys my name was Cock, so now I was known as Cock to everybody. The odd miner turned up at the gypsy site asking how I was. What wonderful men I had around me. The gypsy ladies were kind and loving and looked after me like a son.

Eventually, it was time to leave. Outwardly, the gypsy people showed no feelings or signs of softness. They stored their genuine feelings away—hard surface, soft centre.

Many years afterwards I took over the land next door to the Stag Pub which was an old N.C.B Depot. I fenced it, put 50 tons of crushed stone on the site so it was even and clean, and invited travellers to winter there free of charge. They had showers, toilets, running water, and a gated site, they didn't know me but that wasn't the point; I owed their elders something going back twenty-two years. I never told them about the fight as there was no point, but I saw the same spirit in the younger generation, always scrapping or arranging fights.

Chapter 14

Hotel Cluck

I returned home to coughing Tom and Janet but wasn't the same boy who had left to fight some weeks earlier. I felt uneasy; something had happened to me. I couldn't hear very well from my left side as my eardrum was ruptured from that first blow, also, my hands were stiff and needed more time to heal. The thick bandages around my chest had been removed but my ribs still hurt... but none of these injuries made me uneasy. I just couldn't settle down to everyday work, something had changed in my thought pattern.

While I'd been away, Jersey had asked people who ran businesses and shops if we could work for them and had put my share of the money on one side for me. He did most of the work during my convalescence, and, eventually, I began to settle down. We chatted about the fight and how it had saved our horse and rig. We no longer performed as The Jersey Boys, that enjoyable and entertaining experience was a thing of the past.

I was lucky to have this young man as my friend. He was honest and easy to get along with. We never had a disagreement during our time together.

Both Jersey and Coughing Tom were grateful that we hadn't lost Peter or the rig, but it had taken a terrible fight to safeguard our means of transport.

My friends had kept the businesses going whilst I was out of action. When I arrived home, they threw me a small party and we even had Peter the horse in the back garden so he wouldn't be left out.

Tom owned a small dog, Rex, who loved to sit on Peter's back. The horse didn't mind this, so the dog was lifted up and he sat there in complete contentment. After a while Rex began sleeping with Peter in his stable on a bed of straw covered by a blanket.

Everything was so different now from when I first arrived in Bolton. I had good friends and a good home with plenty of money in constant supply. I was happy and couldn't see this life ever coming to an end. Lots of friendly people greeted me with, 'how are you', or 'good to see you', and there were many homes to visit where I'd be offered a meal and a hot drink. I was welcomed all over Bolton. I was lucky in many ways. During all this time I never wondered who my parents were, and I never thought about London or where I'd come from.

When I awoke in the mornings, my only thoughts were of what I would to do that day. I looked forward to meeting the people with whom I'd come into contact. My mind was always full of planning and involvement. It was exciting, and I can still relate to that. I had no time for thoughts of the past, only of what I was involved with now and going forward.

I didn't know my days in Bolton were to come to an end. Once again, events were out of the hands of the little boy who was now just two months short of his tenth birthday.

My time in Bolton, my experiences, the people with whom I'd shared my life, and the warmth and love I'd been shown by Coughing Tom and Janet and the gypsy people had taught me so much. I believe it better prepared me for later life than a traditional school education and the possession of a school certificate declaring I'd passed English, mathematics, science, and a language would have.

In later life you see more, you understand more. Your thoughts pick out the genuine things, like the people who had nothing to gain by helping a little boy. They involved themselves because they were genuine and their motives were simple.

One such occasion was the time a Lady stopped Jersey and me in the street and asked if we could call around to her terraced house. We left Peter and the rig tethered next to her garden gate and called in to see her.

She welcomed us into her home and began showing us boxes filled with shirts, jumpers, socks, hats, and two or three overcoats. Everything looked brand new and she'd knitted some of the items herself. "Try them on for size" she said. "I want you boys to have them all. I've been told you're both refugees and need looking after."

We tried several things on and although not everything fitted, we were still very happy to have them. We thanked this lovely lady and gave her a few extra coal bricks in return for her kindness.

Tom was surprised when we arrived at the yard with our new woollen hats and scarves. We told him about the generous lady. Tom knew her and told us her husband had been serving in the Navy and was recently killed in action. It seemed she'd kept herself busy knitting things for his return. Sadly, this would never happen. This seemed so sad to Jersey and me. This lovely lady had taken us in and given us all the things she'd made for her husband. She didn't mention him to us. Her thoughts were filled with kindness and how she could help two little refugee boys.

After this amazing act of kindness Janet went to visit this lovely lady every week to keep her company in the evenings.

In those days the streets had gas street lamps. The lamplighter would extinguish the lamps around 9 pm every night and another lamplighter would light them again around 4 am the following morning and extinguish them at 7 am.

It all sounds quite complicated but back then all the street lamps had to be lit and turned off manually. The Lamplighter carried a long pole around with him in order to carry out this tricky procedure.

These people were sometimes referred to as 'Knocker-uppers' because you could make arrangements with them to bang on your front door to wake you for work. This usually took place between 5 and 6 am depending where your house stood on the lamplighter's round. He could earn himself quite a few bob as he went from street to street waking people.

Once, while delivering to the back yard of a terraced house, we noticed a long piece of string hanging down from the upstairs bedroom window.

Jersey and I stared at the string. Unable to restrain his curiosity any longer, my friend gave it a little tug.

We had no way of knowing it was tied to a man's foot and the man was in bed with another man's wife. Apparently, this man and the lamplighter had an arrangement. When he lit the street lamp outside the house at roughly 6 am every morning, the lamplighter would tug on the string to wake the man up, giving him an early warning that his lover's husband was due back from the factory.

However, on this particular morning, the lamplighter had forgotten to pull on the string. It was lucky for the man that Jersey's curiosity had gotten the better of him. At the very moment the young man was walking out of the back door, the husband was coming through the backyard, and Jersey and I were stuck in the middle.

Fortunately for the young man, the husband had just ended a twelve-hour shift and was exhausted and just wanted to get to bed.

He thought the young man was with us delivering coal bricks, and simply said, "How do," and went into the house.

We saw the young man a little later on and he asked us to say nothing about the incident.

He explained the string to us and boasted of his amorous adventures. I've often wondered what would have happened that day if Jersey hadn't pulled the string.

The lady had been a new customer and we had been instructed to deliver no later than 8 am as she'd be out at work after that time. When we returned that evening to collect our payment, she cancelled her account with us and said she was moving out of the area.

Sometimes, when we had early deliveries, we would see the Mill girls, clip clopping in their clogs, along the cobbled streets on their way to work. These strong, hard-working women would walk together arm in arm with shawls over their heads singing the latest tunes by their hero, Gracie Fields. One song I remember hearing many times was 'Sally'. Some of these women worked ten-hour shifts or even longer. I really admired them.

The toneless echo of several thousand pairs of clogs clattering up the damp, cobbled streets was a familiar sound to the people of this era but is one no longer heard in twenty-first century Britain. It's been likened to the cold, hard clatter of horses' hooves on the stones or the march of a cavalry brigade. After a while the mill siren would sound and then, after the last ladies ran through the mill gates trying to avoid a fine for being late to work, the relative silence of the early morning would return.

In the noisy environment of the Mills it was impossible to hear anyone speak, so, the workers developed their own unique sign language which they combined with lip reading. I still remember some of the names given to the various jobs they had to carry out: Doffer, or Under Doffer, Cocker, or Top Cocker to name but a few.

Every now and then the workers were allowed a few days away from work, known as Labour days. The streets would fill with bands and people dancing, marching, and spreads of more food than you can imagine: bread, pies, roasted pig's trotters, cow heal pie, black pudding, tripe, and onions, mountains of freshly cooked Chips, red cabbage, and beetroot—a veritable feast and all homemade.

A particular favourite delicacy was potato pie, red cabbage, jacket potato, and pickled onions followed by Granny Smith's apple pie, all washed down with a flagon of Maggie Marshall's home brewed bitter.

Once the women had downed their bitter, the men seemed to disappear. I often wondered why. No doubt, they were a little frightened of being caught by these local, hardworking factory women.

The old Lancashire saying, 'tha's ow't fer nowt' (meaning, if they didn't earn it, they didn't want it), captures the character of these amazing workers. I really enjoyed this way of life.

Many pensioners, mostly old ladies, wanted half bricks, or a bag of slack (tiny pieces of coal). Often, we saved these small pieces, and, when we became aware that some of these old ladies lived alone with no financial support, we gave the bags away free of charge. In return, we were often invited in and after we had removed our clogs and washed our hands we were treated to a large mug of hot tea and a thick slice of bread and jam.

It was always the same conversation. 'Where do you come from?' 'Where do you live?' 'How long have you been in Bolton?' 'Do you get enough to eat?' and so on and so on.

These old ladies were lonely and having two scruffy rascals to talk to made their day. They loved speaking about their families and departed husbands, and, sometimes, children. Some had lost their husbands in the Great War and their sons in this one. It was rather sad. They always wanted us to stay longer, but we could only chat with them for a short while. We visited at least once a week, but it was always the same conversation: 'Where do you come from?' 'Where do you live?' 'How long have you been in Bolton?' 'Do you get enough to eat?'

Another customer, an elderly gentleman in the truest meaning of the word, lived on his own and he too loved to chat with the little rascals.

One day he invited us into his kitchen and told us he was moving away to live with his sister so had to get rid of his hens— all six of them. She didn't want hens running around her house.

He showed us some fresh eggs and told us the hens laid at least one each a day. Our eyes lit up.

"How much do you want for them," I asked.

"Nothing, at all as long as you look after them and give them a good home."

We arranged for him to come and look at our backyard. He did and was very happy with what he saw. The yard had a straw patch and a garden area where the hens could run around and scratch the ground looking for insects and other things to eat.

Two days later we took him back to our yard. Again, he was very pleased with everything he saw. There was grain for the hens from Peter's nosebag and straw for them to sleep on. They must have thought they'd come to a holiday camp.

Over the next few days we removed the hens from his house and took them to their new home. It all went to plan. They strutted around, finding their favourite spot. Everyone was happy and we promised this kind old gentleman he could have free eggs anytime he came by the yard.

How good was this? We had our very own egg round. All food was rationed yet we had five or six fresh eggs every day.

We kept the first dozen eggs for ourselves and sold the remainder. Early one morning, shortly after the hens came to live with us, I went out into the yard to feed them but could only find four. The following morning there were three. The hens were being stolen at night. Soon we were down to one solitary hen. This was no fox. It was wartime and food was scarce. Someone had discovered our hens and was climbing over the fence at night and stealing them.

To combat this, Tom and Jack built a large chicken coop, with a separate place for hens to sleep and a place to roost, and raised it off the floor to avoid it getting damp. They lined the roof with old, discarded Lino, which at that time was the standard floor covering for most houses. This stopped the rain getting in.

The pals built two doors, one at each end, so food could be placed at one end and the eggs collected from the other. The floor and the nesting area were covered in straw. Tom made the front of the coop out of galvanised netting, there was a large water dish and a small bath area. The remaining hen would have an exercise area and be safe and warm at night.

Our hen took up residence and began laying eggs. Tom named his masterpiece 'Hotel Cluck'.

Jersey and I visited one of our lady pensioners and asked her if she'd come around to the yard. She couldn't walk far, so we came up with the idea of putting a chair on the rig so she could ride around to our yard. This proved to be problematic as we found we couldn't lift her on or off the trailer.

The new coop would hold at least three or four hens, so we asked the gypsy boys for their help. It took them less than a week to provide us with three dark brown hens. They asked us for fifteen pounds to cover the cost of the hens and their time. The birds now installed in the coop, later that day Jersey and I visited the old lady and brought her up to date with our hen story.

We explained we would like her to look after the new hen house and the four hens. We would set it up in her back yard and put netting around it to keep them from escaping. Also, we would come around once a week and provide fresh straw, hen food, and grain, and clean the area and take away the rubbish.

"The hens will lay around twenty eggs every week," I said, "and you can keep seven for yourself. You can have a fresh egg every day."

Jersey added, "Looking after them will be company too."

Our story sounded good, but she just looked at us and never said a word. Eventually she agreed to a two-month trial, as long as we did what we had promised.

Jersey and I glanced at each other and smiled. We fetched the coop and set it up in her garden installing the hens and netting as promised.

We noticed an amazing change in this old lady. The birds bonded with her and she became a real mother to them. When the sun was out, she sat outside in a comfortable chair talking to them and throwing grain on the soft earth.

Once a week we cleaned around the henhouse, refilled the water tray, took away the old straw, provided fresh bedding, and collected whatever eggs the old lady had for us. This took around twenty minutes. Afterwards we sat with her and had a hot cup of tea and a slice of bread and jam. As she got to know each individual hen, she told us which the boss was, and which ate more than the others and so on. Of course, she was rewarded with fresh eggs from Hotel Cluck.

This small investment proved to be great value for money and gave us plenty of fresh eggs every week.

Our venture was a success and the old lady's neighbours didn't mind hearing the clucking in the mornings; they received eggs, and their children were welcomed into the garden to help feed the hens. That was the story of Hotel Cluck.

Chapter 15

Irish Pat from Tipperary

One day we had a visit from a tall, stocky gypsy lad who spoke with a strange accent. He told Coughing Tom he wanted to see me. So, Tom made him a mug of tea while they waited for Jersey and me to return.

When we got back from town the lad introduced himself as Patrick and told us he'd just arrived from County Tipperary in Ireland. The other Gypsies had said we would find him accommodation and work. At first, we were unsure what to do with him. Here he was with no home, no money, and no friends.

He told us he was a fist fighter and asked if we could arrange Fights for him. Tom got involved with the conversation and it was agreed Patrick, or Pat as we called him, could sleep in the stable for a few nights with Peter the horse, and Janet would send food down for him until we could find him somewhere more permanent.

Patrick agreed to Tom's suggestion. I went with Jersey to the gypsy camp to find out who the lad was and why he'd been directed to us instead of being invited to stay at their camp.

The head gypsy wore a bright green waistcoat. When he saw me, he took hold of me and gave me a huge hug. He called for his wife, who came running and kissed my forehead then ran off. She returned with hot tea and bread and cheese.

I learned that the Irish lad couldn't stay with the Gypsies because his father had run off with a gypsy girl without the consent of her family. He was a bad egg and had moved back to Ireland. All this happened several years ago, but, as a result, they wouldn't let Pat stay with them. It was a great shame as he'd done nothing wrong. It was a case of the sins of the father being visited on the son.

Pat had gained quite a reputation as a fighter and had never lost a fight. Now, with the fighting name of 'Irish Pat from Tipperary' he was prepared to fight for money in what was known to the Gypsies as 'The Blood Tub'.

The head gypsy told me, "Look after him. I'll arrange him fights around local farms and warehouses."

On my return home, I filled Tom in on what I'd learned. He suggested I tell Pat, which I did. The lad was delighted. Now we had a fighting gypsy to manage. You could almost say 'hens out, Gypsies in'.

We made him a bed in the stable, gave him several buckets of warm water, and hung a cover around him for privacy so he could have a strip down wash with green carbolic soap.

Tom gave him a clean shirt and socks. In time we got him a pair of boots, a thick coat, jumper, toothpaste, and brush. Prior to this he'd used black soot to clean his teeth. Coughing Tom made him a punchbag from an old potato sack filled with earth and hung it over a beam in the stable for him to practice on. There was, however, a problem. This lad could eat, and we struggled to keep up with his appetite. I'm sure he could eat as much as an elephant. After a while we had to take him to Bolton market and find him work so they could feed him.

One day, we received instructions for us all to go to a warehouse, the venue for his first fight. It would be on a basis of 'winner takes all'. The prize was ten pounds which was a lot of money in those days. The winner would also keep what was known as 'nubbins'— the spare change thrown into the ring by spectators if they considered it a good fight.

Tom showed us the way and off we went with our full rig and our Irish prize fighter who sat silently all the way, deep in thought. I grinned and chatted, excited as we stepped into the unknown. Another adventure awaited us.

When we arrived at the warehouse a gypsy man walked over, wished us well, and gave Tom a cigar. I recognised the man from my time staying at the camp.

He escorted us to an area at the side of the warehouse where the fighters got ready. We thought the action would begin right away but were told there were two fights scheduled before Irish Pat would go into the ring. He showed our fighter several gloves of varying sizes. These were not the traditional boxing gloves of today but were cloth gloves with a little padding over the knuckles.

Still silent, Pat tried a pair on. He seemed happy with these and said he was ready. There was no other boxing attire to wear, just good boots and thick trousers. Nothing else was allowed.

Tom smeared cream around Pat's eyes and nose, and we placed our coats over his shoulders to keep him warm. This was a good move; an hour later we were still waiting to be called into the warehouse.

Eventually the shouting and cheering in the warehouse died down and a man came out and beckoned us inside. It was time for Irish Pat to step up to the mark.

"Everything okay?" I asked him. "You ready?"

He nodded. "You should be asking my opponent if he's ready for a sleep."

Two hundred pairs of eyes settled on us as we stepped into the building. The shouting, the cheers, the smell of sweat, liniment, and cigarettes hung in the air. I glanced at the rough, tough men taking one or two hundred-pound bets from each other. There were no bookies, that was illegal, the shake of a hand completed each transaction, and no one would renege on the hurried agreement—it was a matter of honour. I smiled as I looked to our little group, proud we were managing our very own fighting man from Ireland. I was so excited I found it difficult to breathe.

A tall, well-built man walked past the crowd and led us to the ring.

Pat calmly stepped over the ropes and onto the canvass and took a long deep breath. Another man announced this would be a fight to the finish. I guessed this meant last man standing.

Tom stepped into Pat's corner with a bucket of water, a towel, and a sponge.

The announcer introduced Sailor Jack to the cheering crowd. "This fighter has won over two hundred fights."

Sailor Jack stepped into the ring. My mouth dropped open. Head and shoulders taller than Pat, and with tattoos all over his body, he formed two white knuckle fists and swung his huge arms in front of his enormous barrel chest. It frightened me to just look at him, but his appearance didn't faze Pat.

Each man went to their corner and waited for the bell to sound and the fight to begin.

Clang. They sprung out of their corners and approached each other in the centre of the ring, their hands help up in fighter position. The big sailor took an almighty swing at Pat.

Pat stepped to one side. The blow missed him.

Our man quickly stepped back and caught the challenger a crunching blow to the ribs. The sailor gasped, winded, unable to return a punch. Pat delivered a devastating thwack to his opponent's head.

Sailor Jack fell on the solid flooring like a sack of potatoes. The fight was over. A powerful, well aimed left, and a solid right from Irish Pat were all it took to floor the huge man.

The crowd, which were mainly Gypsies, cheered, shouted, and shook their fists in the air—a thunderous reception. They threw money into the ring from all sides while Sailor Jack still lay stone cold on the floor. No one counted to ten, under these rules there was no count.

Tom took Pat to his corner and signalled Jersey and me to collect the money thrown in the ring and the winner's prize of ten pounds. I glanced at the tattooed fighter. He was still lying motionless.

Irish Pat, the lad who had been forbidden to stay with his people, was the hero of the night. As we walked back to our makeshift dressing room, the gypsy men crowded around him pushing notes and coins into his hands.

We walked back to our rig where a few more gypsy men waited for us. They wanted to congratulate the winner, shake him by the hand, and give him more money.

The men invited us back to their camp for a party. So off we went, and all the while Irish Pat said nothing.

What a punch this young man had—the speed, the power, and an ice-cold attitude. Where had he got such talent? Sometime later, we learnt our hero was only eighteen years old. He'd begun fighting other gypsy boys back in Ireland at the tender age of seven.

We accompanied him to six further fights, and he won them all. By now his prize money had reached fifty pounds per fight plus all the nubbins thrown into the ring out of appreciation for his great fighting talent.

How things had changed for him since the day he came looking for us with nowhere to sleep or wash and with nothing to eat.

But it all ended one day when he said goodbye. Before leaving, he handed twenty pounds each to Janet and Tom.

Jersey and I only received a handshake, but it didn't matter to us. Meeting and spending time with this young man was worth more than money.

Later still, we learned he'd made quite a bit of money and returned to Ireland, married a Gypsy girl, and bought a farm in Tipperary called "Clonmell."

Chapter 16

Our Holiday

On Friday afternoons, we gathered in the yard to count the week's earnings and work out our overheads.

This particular Friday, someone at our last delivery gave us a huge dish of potato pie with cabbage and other vegetables. There was enough for everyone.

Of course, Peter was always included in our Friday lunches and received an extra treat. After giving him a complete wash down, scrubbing his hooves and legs, we plaited his tail, combed his mane, and took him to Quibeck fields. There, we tethered him on a long rope thus allowing him to munch away on the fresh grass for a couple of hours. He loved this and everybody loved Peter. When we returned our food was ready and our weekly meeting began.

We took the potato pie to the camp fire and sat with Tom and Jack. Out came the tin plates and mugs. Our large black kettle boiled on the fire ready for our tea and the Coughing Twins toasted thick slices of bread over the flames on long metal toasting forks. A large bowl of dripping sat ready for our Friday afternoon feast. This was our Director's boardroom meeting.

I loved the wonderful life we had created through hard work and honest friendship. During the conversation, Tom suggested Janet needed a holiday and we should all go away together.

"Blackpool would be my choice," he said. "What do you think of that?" Jersey and I frowned. We'd never had a holiday.

"What's a holiday?" I asked. "What do you do on holiday? What's it for?"

"You go on holiday to have fun," Tom told us. "You can swim in the sea, walk on the beach, have Donkey rides, eat Blackpool rock, and have rides on the funfair."

This seemed a little strange to a young boy who couldn't swim, had never seen a beach, and certainly had never heard of anyone eating rock. Neither Jersey nor I knew what a funfair was and why, we wondered, would we want to ride on a donkey when we had lovely Peter to ride every day?

We thought about it for a moment then shook our heads. I spoke for us both. "We don't think much of the idea."

However, Tom wouldn't hear of it and said Janet would never go on holiday without us. Finally, we agreed to go. Tom would make the arrangements.

Peter had to be considered too. We couldn't take him on Holiday. He'd need looking after whilst we were away, and the yard had to be taken care of and coal-bricks manufactured.

Tom and Janet got on with sorting everything out and explained it all to Jersey and me. Okay *I thought, we'll go to Blackpool, eat rock, walk on the beach, and paddle in the sea, but we won't ride Donkeys or go on the funfair.*

"You and Jersey will have a great time," Janet told us.

Neither of us liked the idea, but we kept quiet so we didn't upset Janet or Coughing Tom. They had been so good to us.

On the day we were scheduled to leave, we walked to Bolton train station and crammed into the overcrowded train. The thick black engine smoke got into my nose and lungs, and made several people cough, nevertheless, they chatted and giggled in excitement at the prospect of going to Blackpool. Jersey and I still didn't really understand what was happening but tried to make the best of it.

About an hour later, the train pulled into Blackpool station, filled to the gunnels with very excited holiday makers.

Everyone expected to have a good time. The mills and factories were closed for two weeks, known as 'wake weeks', and the workers were using the free time for fun and refreshment. Despite our earlier reservations, Jersey and I found ourselves getting caught up in the excitement and expectation.

When we reached Blackpool town centre my mouth dropped open. My young friend and I had never seen anywhere like this before. To a small lad it was a wonderland of fun and noise and strange, sweet smells, and a sharp contrast to our home town. How could this place be so different? It was only a short train journey away from Bolton.

We walked to the self-contained flat where Tom and Janet had arranged for us to stay. It belonged to two of their friends and was near the seafront. When I opened my bedroom window, I could smell the sea air and hear the seagulls screeching overhead. The rented accommodation was bigger than our house back in Bolton. I grinned and began to think I'd enjoy being on holiday.

There were three bedrooms, an indoor bathroom, a large lounge with dining area, and a fitted kitchen. There was even a telephone, which was nice, but not much good to us as none of us had anyone to ring. We didn't know anyone with a telephone.

This holiday idea was beginning to appeal to me. Maybe we should have lots more of these trips to Blackpool.

Our first outing was a walk along the seafront. There was so much to see: waves lapping on the sandy beach, crowds of holiday makers sitting in deckchairs, (most wearing day clothes rather than the skimpy swimwear of the twenty-first century,) donkeys giving rides to children and young people, ice cream tenders selling their wares, roadside stalls filled to overflowing with sweets of every colour and shape, side show attractions, the tower looming overhead...

Jersey and I walked around wide-eyed, our mouths dropping open at the different sights. As the mills and factories all closed at the same time and the workers all poured into Blackpool, everybody seemed to know one another. They smiled, laughed, and shouted to each other, relaxed after their hard year's work. Children ran around, playing, eating toffee apples, and kicking footballs on the beach. Some of my old customers from Bolton recognised Jersey and me and came over to shake our hands and give us huge hugs.

There were so many fascinating things going on around us. A lady stood behind a small machine selling what appeared to be large balls of pink cotton wool which you could eat. Tom told us it was called candy floss. We came across a large dummy in a glass box, and when you put a penny in the slot, he laughed very loudly. This drew a small crowd who began to laugh too.

Further along the promenade, amongst the sprawling shops, tents, and marquees, was a large round building filled with excited holiday makers playing 'Housey House', a popular game now known as bingo.

We were totally mesmerised by this exciting wonderland full of noise and strange smells of food cooking in side kiosks. There was food everywhere. Back home, we could only buy food when we presented our ration cards or sweet coupons. Here, food flowed freely. The contrast felt strange.

I asked Tom and Janet, "Do we have to give our ration books to buy the food?"

They both laughed. Janet said, "No. We can buy everything with the money we brought with us."

Later, Tom told us we were going to a place called 'Woolworths' to eat fish and chips in the restaurant. *A restaurant?* I thought. *What's that?* Jersey and I had never heard of a restaurant. We only ever went to the local UCP shop.

We set out along the promenade watching the sea lapping on the beach on our one side and looking at the several small kiosks and shops on the other. Each offered tempting delights such as ice cream in cornets, or hot dogs and fried onions, winkles, fudge, and hard Blackpool rock to the passing holiday crowd.

Along the way, a lady sat in front of a small tent with the front tied open. When she saw me she stood up and waved. I could see she was a gypsy, but she looked different to my gypsy friends back home. She wore a scarf around her head, hooped earrings, and her neck was decked in jewellery. Her fingers were bejeweled with rings and several shiny bangles caught the sun as she moved her arms. Her dress was bright Red and sparkled.

She walked towards me; her deep brown eyes boring into me. I stood still, a slight quiver of unease in my stomach, and she reached out and placed her right hand on my shoulder and her left hand on my head.

Her voice was deep, and she spoke with a strange accent. "How are you? Do you still have any pain in your chest?

"Yes," I answered.

"Where are you going?"

Tom spoke. "We're going for fish and chips at Woolworths."

The bejeweled lady looked towards Tom. "Go without the lad and come back for him in about half an hour."

Tom and Janet glanced at each other and back to the lady. Tom said, "No. We can't leave the lad."

She stepped back towards the tent, her hand still on my head, and asked me, "Have you recovered from your fight?"

I said, "Nearly." I was confused. How did this stranger, know about my fight or my injuries? (To this day, I still have no idea.)

"Your grandfather came from Ireland. You have his eyes." She took her hand off my head, opened both my hands, and pointed to my little fingers. "Your left finger has four pads, but your right finger only has three. This trait comes from your grandmother. She'd exactly the same odd pads on her little fingers. Can you hold your hands together as though you're praying?" I did so.

She looked at the edges of my hands and then turned towards Tom and asked him again, "Can you let the lad stay with me for about half an hour?" Tom and Janet refused, so she turned back to me and looked again at the edges of my hands, which I was still holding up as though praying.

101

She smiled. "You have nothing to worry about in life. You'll never be short of money and will employ many people through the many business's you will have." She paused. "Your mother has been crying a lot because you were taken from her, and she is trying to find you."

She kissed me on the forehead, thanked me, and wished me well. I frowned. How could this gypsy lady, working in a tent in Blackpool, know all these things? I've often wondered what she might have told me if Tom and Janet had let me stay for that half hour.

We left the lady and went for our fish and chips, and I never saw her again.

The newly opened Woolworth Building stood near Blackpool Tower on Bank Hey Street. It boasted a massive tower with a large clock on the front. The huge premises dominated the skyline, and, I'm told, was visible for miles along the Fylde coast and right out to sea. I stared at the glazed, cream bricks and bronze window frames until Jersey nudged me and then I followed Tom and Janet inside. The restaurant was huge and very fancy. I'd never seen such a beautiful building.

Woolworths offered main dishes for sixpence (two-and-a-half pence in today's money) and a full meal for two shillings or less (ten pence). Waiters and waitresses buzzed around clearing tables, and families with small children sat chatting and enjoying the food. Nearly all the tables were taken, but we found a free one and ordered fish, chips, peas, bread and butter, and four large mugs of hot steaming tea.

***

I'd had a wonderful time and had enjoyed many new experiences, but I didn't return to Blackpool until June 2016. That day, after a successful business meeting, I went for a walk and tried to find the old Woolworths' Building. I walked along Central Pier for a short time and there it was, still standing: the building, tower, and the clock. However, the Woolworths sign had gone, and the clock wasn't working.

Many shops had closed and had metal shutters over the windows, and the buildings looked tired and dirty. I wondered what had become of the gypsy lady who seemed to know all about me and my family.

How things had changed in 75 years.

***

We passed our time away that summer, so long ago, walking along the beach, hiring rowing boats, eating candy floss, and taking horse and carriage rides along the promenade. Another day, we went to the top of the famous tower. I stood on the balcony and took a deep breath as the wind buffeted my young face. I could see for miles and miles... rows and rows of houses, people as small as ants, cars driving along the promenade, tiny waves crashing on the beach.

After coming back down in the lift, we visited the Zoo situated under the tower. I didn't like this; the animals were confined in cages too small for them to walk around.

Later, we visited the ice-skating show and went to look at the piers that jutted out, for what seemed miles, into the Irish Sea. Each had shows, shops, and stalls to entice the holiday makers to part with their hard-earned money. I particularly liked the Punch and Judy shows which always attracted large crowds. We saw the World's most tattooed lady and met Tommy Farr, a Welsh, ex-Heavyweight boxer, who had been to America to fight for the World Heavyweight Championship. He spoke in an accent that reminded me of the Welsh man I'd lived with in Fultham.

As the days passed, we got into a routine. Morning began with a hearty breakfast, then Janet prepared sandwiches and cakes, and two large flasks of tea for our day on the beach.

Tom and Janet hired deckchairs and sunbathed in the warm sunshine. Every day, they were asleep within minutes, so Jersey and I left them to their slumber and headed off to explore more of the delights and surprises Blackpool had to offer. These were fun-filled days; two young lads running around and exploring the town as free as the wind.

One day we caught a tram to Bispham, a town further along the promenade. We were unimpressed with this sleepy town and soon headed back to the thrills and spills of Blackpool.

Often upon returning from our adventures, Jersey and I'd find Tom and Janet still fast asleep in their deckchairs. They needed the rest and certainly deserved it.

Too soon, our holiday came to an end and the time came to board the overcrowded train and head back to Bolton. Although the holiday was ending, Jersey and I couldn't wait to see Peter again and to find out how the business was doing.

Chapter 17

The Return

A few months after the holiday, we went out to deliver coal-bricks. A few local miners had started getting free coal and were selling it, so we reduced the price of our bricks back to three-pence a brick and a penny ha'penny for a broken half.

While we were leading Peter along the road, a lad we knew came running up and said the school inspector was at our front door and Janet was outside crying.

I jumped off the rig and said to Jersey, "Follow me in five minutes, but keep a distance. We can't let anyone official see the rig."

I ran back and rounded the corner of our street. Janet and a man stood outside the house. I walked up to them. Janet saw me first.

She wiped her eyes. "I want you to meet someone. This is your father, and you're going home to London."

The man studied me and spoke in a London accent. "Hello, Son."

I gasped. My heart raced and a sudden coldness hit the core of my being. I wanted to run away back 'round the corner to Jersey and hide. I didn't know this man; he was a stranger. Why should I go to London? My life, my business, my friends, my family, everything was here with me in Bolton. What right did this stranger have to tear me away from everything?

I shook my head. "I'm not going to London. I live here. I don't live in London."

The man, took a deep breath, surprised at my answer. "I'm your father. You have to come back to London with me now."

Jersey arrived in the rig, and on hearing what was happening he ran back up the road and told Coughing Tom, "Little Cock's going home."

Coughing Tom marched up the road with Jersey in tow.

Tom's voice was controlled and serious "You're not going anywhere."

An official stepped out of a car which had parked across the road and showed Tom and Janet the papers that stated I had to leave with my father.

Tom couldn't accept this. He shook his head. "You're not going."

A neighbour stepped out of her house and joined in the argument. "No, the lad lives here."

Another neighbour tried to pull me into her house. By now Tom, Janet, and I were crying.

My father was a quiet man and didn't like being stuck in the middle of the awkward situation. He'd travelled on a train all the way from Tooting and was tired out and now standing in the middle of conflict. He'd probably thought I'd be delighted to see him and would have thrown my belongings into a bag and left with him.

There was no escaping the inevitable. Just as in my ereption from Mrs Plumbridge's home, my wishes were not taken into consideration; the law was the law. I had to leave with the stranger and go to London.

Because I'd just returned from my rounds selling coal bricks, I was covered in coal dust. The official and my father waited for me outside on the pavement while I had a wash and clean up in the bathroom. Coughing Tom, Janet, Jersey, and I said a tearful goodbye. I ran into the back yard to say my good byes to Peter, then I got into the car with my head bowed and a heavy weight in my heart, and that was the last time I saw any of them.

My share of the business, money, everything, was gone, my friends, life, and the home where I'd been so happy were now just memories in a little boy's mind.

I travelled to London with my father in complete silence, then we boarded a tube train, and afterwards took a twenty-minute walk. And at approximately two in the morning, still shocked and angry at the injustice life had once again served me, I arrived outside a house in Tooting of which I held no recollection.

My father opened the front door, and we stepped inside the hallway.

A lady came running down the stairs shouting, "My baby, my baby," then stopped when she saw a ten-year-old boy she didn't recognise standing in front of her.

My mother was in shock. I'd left home aged three years and eight months to go to see the ducks—and I'd seen plenty of those in every county in England. What did we have in common? What was there to talk about?

Father put the kettle on, and a teenage girl appeared—the same girl who was supposed to hold my hand and never let go.

She said, "Hello. How are you?"

I stood there, my face ashen and my eyes hard. I looked from my sister to my mother, then to my father, and back to my sister.

Finally, I said, "Yes, I'm ok. I saw the ducks..."

I thought, *I've seen it, done it, learned it, forgotten it, sold it. I've lived a life on my own moving from place to place with no help from you... and never asked for any. I don't want any now, so, how are you?!*

Part 2

Chapter 18

Inner Rage

I had returned to my family home unsure of my exact age. For years I'd not known my date of birth or even the month of my birthday. Living as I had, age and birthdays weren't important.

Being ripped from my happy home in Bolton and being forced to live with strangers with whom I had nothing in common, left me in shock and in a very dark place in my mind. I can't adequately describe my feelings except to say I was giddy with rage. I wanted to cry for my lost home; I wanted to be with my friends; I wanted my business. What was I doing here, in Tooting... in this house? What was I doing with these people? I didn't know them, and I didn't want to know them. My mind screamed, *please, please let me go... let me go back to my home and my life.* These thoughts spun around and around in my head.

I heard my genetic family speaking, but their conversations were of no interest to me and I found their constant questions and the attention they gave me annoying. My stomach was in knots. I wanted to hit something. What could I do? How could I escape the torture in my mind and body? The frustration grew; I knew I couldn't leave the house—I'd be lost in street after street of terraced houses. They all looked the same. When I stepped outside, I saw unfamiliar streets and big red buses with large numbers on the back and fronts passing in every direction, one after another.

Who would know the way to Bolton? Who could I ask?

I spotted a man with a horse and cart delivering milk—at last a familiar sight—maybe he would know. I walked across the road and asked him.

The man frowned and looked down at me. "You speak with a funny accent. Where's Bolton?"

"In Lancashire," I said.

The man laughed and the empty bottles chinked as he placed them back in their crates, then without telling me what I wanted to know he left to deliver more milk.

My parents enrolled me in a local school. I went along and was given a test. I hadn't been in education for a long time, so, except for the arithmetic questions, didn't do well. I could have answered questions on coal bricks and horses and even on fighting and learning to survive on my own, but there were no such questions on the test.

My mother informed the headmaster I'd been away and had just returned. Still not wanting to be in London or in school, someone placed me in a class with boys and girls who all spoke in London accents. I didn't like this and couldn't understand what they were saying. The teacher had me stand at the front of the class facing the children so I could be introduced to everyone. He told them I was from Lancashire and asked me to describe Bolton.

As soon as I spoke, a boy began mimicking my accent. "Bolton... Bolton..."

I wasn't in the mood to be the butt of his joke and have the class laughing at me.

I marched down the aisle between the rows of desks and punched the boy in the face. He fell backwards, so I kicked him in the body and head. I'd found a place to vent some of my built-up anger. I was a fighter. I'd fought a lad older than myself by gypsy rules. This boy didn't stand a chance—none of them did. The teacher came up behind me, took hold of me around the neck with his arm, and dragged me outside the classroom, so I kicked him too.

A bigger boy stepped into the hall and ran over and grabbed me around the neck from one side. He forced my head down between his elbow and the side of his body in a headlock and thumped me in the face a couple times. I punched him in the groin, wriggled free, and got in a few good punches. His lip split and blood dripped from his nose.

I left the school by the side door and walked to the shops. My life was not in Tooting and never would be.

Some hours later, I returned to my parents' house. Mum told me the police had called, and my father had instructions to take me to the police station.

At around five feet tall, Father was a small, placid man with no temper at all. He was an artist not a fighter. He looked at me and spoke calmly telling me we had to go to the station right away, and so I obeyed him. We walked to the station at Amen-Corner.

We stepped inside and my father told the receptionist who we were, and a police officer showed us both into an interview room where we sat behind a desk. A few minutes later another law enforcement officer strode into the room, asked my name, and reprimanded me. He wasn't taking any fuss and considered this a serious offence.

He looked me straight in the eye, his voice loud and stern. "The boy you attacked was taken to hospital." The police officer looked at my father. "His parents called in here and reported the crime." Dad shook his head. The blood had drained from his face. The officer looked back to me, "We'll find out the extent of the boy's injuries later this evening. Then we'll let you know what you'll be charged with. The boy's parents are coming back to see you too."

A policeman escorted my father and me to a room and told us to wait there for the outcome. None of this bothered me at all. We sat and waited. My father said little, but I guessed he wished he'd left me in Bolton.

During our wait one or two people came into the room and spoke to my father. Each gave me long looks. Eventually, someone led us into another room where we took another seat.

The door opened and the original police officer led in a man and a lady. They stared at me. I felt a quiver in my stomach and shifted in my seat.

The man said something to my father and pointed at me. I didn't hear him properly so asked my dad what he'd said.

Dad repeated it. "Your son can only hit my son when he's sitting down. That's what cowards do."

Dad was pale and had a slight quiver in his voice. He'd never been to a police station before and had no experience of violence or fighting. I asked him if he was okay. For the first time, I felt a bond with this little man. I stood up to go; I'd had enough of this.

The police officer's voice was still firm. "Sit down. Someone's coming to see you."

I told him, "My dad had nothing to do with this and has to go home. I only met him a few days ago."

The second officer stood up and took him to another room and gave him a cup of tea. I later learned the policeman questioned him about me.

After the boy's parents had glared at me for a while longer, another man stepped in with a report. He placed it on the table in front of the first officer who looked down at it.

He spoke to the parents. "It says here, your son has sustained no real damage, so you can leave."

The lad's father stood up and strode over to me speaking and wagging his finger. The rage stirred up inside me, so spat in his face and took a swing at him.

He jumped back in shock. The police officer grabbed me and pulled me over to the far side of the room. Dad was upset, and I felt sorry I'd involved him in the rough side of life. I'd been looking after myself for the last six years. This world was foreign to him.

111

The boy's parents hurried out of the room and the officer released me. Now two more men joined us.

The first man spoke to my father. "You'll receive paperwork explaining your son has to appear at Brixton Juvenile Court for corrective training. It'll be on a Saturday."

The second man asked me, "Have you done any boxing or been a member of a club?"

I shook my head. "No. I've been busy making coal-bricks. How much do you get paid for a fight?"

He didn't answer. Both men took my dad into the other room to finish his cup of tea. A few minutes later they came back and took me to the police gymnasium at the far end of the station. A few men were jumping around boxing while others punched large bags hanging from hooks. Nearer to where I was standing two boys moved around a boxing ring taking what I considered to be half-hearted punches at each other. They wore large, padded gloves—not like the ones the gypsy fighters wore. The other big difference was the gypsy boys stood toe to toe for the fight and didn't dance around the ring.

One man asked, "Would you like to join the club?"

"I don't dance around with big gloves on when I fight."

The man paused before speaking. "Your father has been taken home. He wasn't well."

The other man said, "If you have a go you might feel better. Would you like a spat with one of the junior boxing team? They won't hurt you."

I stood still for a moment while I considered my answer. My hobnail boots weren't suitable for the ring.

I took off my coat and jumper and put on two gloves that reached halfway up my forearms and entered the ring still wearing my big black boots. I walked to the centre waiting for a toe to toe, but the other lad danced about all over the place, throwing out punches and dancing away.

This was brilliant, like a game of hit and run. I stood still watching for my chance. It soon came. I ducked under my opponent's glove and struck him with a right hook straight under his chin. He fell back to the ropes, so I followed up with what is known in Lancashire as a Leeds kiss: a head butt to the nose.

The man who had suggested I have this fight pulled me out of the ring. "You're a street fighter, not a boxer. Go to Mitcham green where the gypsy boys have blood-tub fights for money."

My heart sank. I'd felt good in the ring and was just getting started; it was a pity it finished so quickly.

A few Saturdays later, my mother took me to Brixton Juvenile Court. The boy I'd beaten up was there with his parents. They kept away from me, which was a good thing for them. The man in charge, probably the magistrate, said I now had a blot on my character. I understood none of that and kept asking my mother where the blot was.

The local school wouldn't accept me because of the blot and because my last visit there had ended in a ban from the premises after only ninety minutes.

Instead, because my grandmother was Catholic, my father enrolled me in a Catholic school. I would only be there a year and would have to take the eleven plus exam. By now I could read and write, and, due to my stairs education in Devon, my arithmetic was the best in the class.

I was called in to see the headmaster with my mother present. He informed us I'd come top in arithmetic but near the bottom in everything else, and one subject wouldn't gain me entrance to a grammar school. It was a great shame I hadn't studied any other subjects. Consequently, I was enrolled into a secondary modern school. (Up to the age of eleven I'd only attended school for a total of two-and-a-half years.)

However, I had many ideas of how to earn money. This is how my mind worked—and I didn't earn any money by going to school. I'd noticed several things I could do to earn a profit. One of them was to take on a paper round before school hours, but there wasn't much money in that, so I worked out a scheme with the newspapers that no one had thought of.

113

I visited Ports, a local newsagent on Fransician Road, noting it closed at 6pm.

"What do you do with the unsold papers?" I asked the shopkeeper.

The man stared at me. "They're collected in the morning to be recycled and shredded."

I offered him a penny a paper for them all and we did a deal on the spot.

After borrowing three pounds from the lady who lived next door, I returned to the shop with a small barrow and purchased twenty-six newspapers. This came to one pound two shillings. I placed them in the barrow and pushed it to Tooting Broadway tube station, and, after I had sold papers there, I moved on to the tram stop. Both sites were busy, packed with those travelling to work or on their way home: a paper to read on the train or an evening paper to take home was most welcome, and I sold most of my papers within the hour. It felt like old times again.

Next, I wheeled my barrow to the Granada Cinema—a short walk away—and sold the papers to those queueing outside. I sold the rest outside various pubs. By 8 pm my barrow was empty, and I'd made two pounds profit. I was working for about a pound an hour. I considered my options. If I extended my hours, I could raise this amount to two pounds ten shillings per night.

I couldn't start work before 6.30 pm and my mother wanted me home by 9 pm so I would have to finish by 8.30 pm— this only allowed me two hours. The restriction was no good for business so after a week I gave up on this venture. I'd made a few pounds and repaid my neighbour but was looking for another earner.

A local shop in Tooting Broadway sold all sizes of coloured beads. They captured my imagination; I'd never before see anything like them. I bought a selection, a ball of strong thread, and some small, black presentation boxes and took them to Mrs Miller, an old lady for whom I ran errands. She agreed to thread them together to make bracelets and matching necklaces.

They looked tremendous. Fashion was just getting going after the war, so I took them to a jewellers in their presentation boxes. They bought them off me. I made one-pound profit on every necklace and ten shillings (equivalent to fifty pence) on the wrist bracelets.

My sister, Alice, became interested in my new venture and tied bows around the boxes. This set them off nicely. She sold several to her friends and got involved in the manufacturing and spent more and more time designing other fashion products. Our project was now well underway and was a great success.

I stumbled upon another project, this time involving men's clothing. One Saturday I visited a large, men's outfitters. The tailoring, which was completed to a high standard, was carried out in the North of England, but the display jackets sitting on the window dummies had no lining.

I walked across to the assistant and asked, "Why aren't the window jackets finished?"

She told me, "Jackets and coats displayed in windows catch the sun and fade. We can't sell them so there's no point going to the expense of adding a lining."

"So, what happens to them?"

"We dispose of them."

I saw a money-making opportunity here and asked the manager if he had any jackets or coats waiting for disposal. He frowned at the young lad asking such an unusual question and said he had. He must have thought this a good idea because he went into the stock room and returned with two jackets which he sold me for two pounds each. As expected, they were fully tailored and just needed lining. I thanked the manager and left.

I showed these to Mrs Gooders, a lady who worked from home altering all kinds of clothing.

"These are excellent," she said, taking a jacket from me. "I can feel the quality... and look at that workmanship. I can line these, but the lining won't be expensive."

I smiled. "Great."

"I'll buy labels too and sew them in."

We checked the jackets over for 'sunburn' but found none and agreed I'd pay her two pounds per jacket—so the two jackets now stood me at four pounds ten shillings per jacket.

I was excited to see the finished articles and was not disappointed. Mrs Gooders had steam-cleaned both jackets, and each were waiting for me on hangers inside a brown bag.

I asked how much I'd expect to get for them at sale. She told me her price was private, but she'd pay me eight pounds per jacket after sale. The only proviso was that I pay her for her work before the sale. I did so, and this left me a profit of three pounds ten shillings per item—a good deal all round.

One week later, I called at her house and was pleased to discover she'd sold both jackets and had new customers waiting for more.

I returned to the clothing shop. The manager led me into the stockroom where long rows of coats and jackets hung on hangers.

He said, "You can pick out whatever you want." These items had no lining, but that was the whole point of my venture. I checked through the stock and picked out five jackets which cost me ten pounds. My only problem now was transporting the said jackets to the tailor's.

Taking a taxi would cost me three pounds and would have to be deducted from my profit. Mrs Gooders picked out four jackets which she said she could sell and told me I'd have to sell the other one myself. This didn't bother me. I had plenty of time in which to sell the odd jacket.

Seven days later, I called back and paid her the seven pounds I owed her for the work. Three days later she'd sold three jackets and completed the remaining two—which she now wanted to sell herself. She owed me twenty-four pounds; I owed her five pounds. We settled up leaving me a profit of seventeen pounds ten shillings, less three pounds for the taxi.

The average wage in 1947 for a forty-six-hour week was nine to ten pounds and I'd made a profit of fourteen pounds. During my taxi journeys to the tailor's house I saw many of the boys who had passed their eleven plus exam walking home from school. They looked grand in their long trousers, jackets and matching hats. Each carried large bags full of homework. I was glad I wasn't tied up with homework and could do what I did best: make money.

Alice was very involved with the fancy necklace making business and was earning money for the both of us, and my jacket lining business was doing well. I was managing four or five jackets every week, and when my supplier ran short of stock, the manager made arrangements with another store to send their jackets over. There was seldom a shortage.

One Saturday, I arrived at the shop at 5pm, the usual time. A lady showed me into the small staff room. The old manager had been replaced. This new manager stared at me straight-faced and asked what was going on with the jacket business.

I told him everything had been paid for and asked if there was a problem. He told me no more jackets would be for sale— one door opens, another door closes. I made enquiries at other stores but found no success. Mrs Gooders was upset at the sudden let down of supply, but I could do nothing about it.

Chapter 19

Back in Business

Two years had passed since my return home to Tooting. Although I wasn't making a fortune, I made sure my mother was never short of money. For some time now I'd been considering selling in the school playground. The children were out there three times a day: morning, lunchtime, and at afternoon breaks. I reasoned that all those boys had pocket money to spend. I had an idea and had to try it.

The following Saturday morning I visited Blooms, a Jewish sweet manufacturer, and asked if I could buy the large jars or any sweets that had been returned or wouldn't sell.

Due to my age, I didn't get a good reception.

The man stared at me. "Who are you? What's that all about? Who told you to make enquiries?" He shot more questions at me then pointed me toward another outlet.

I made inquiries there but got no further. They wouldn't sell to me because I was too young, and I lacked the evidence of being a registered shop or business.

(Sweets had only just come off rationing. In total, food rationing in Britain lasted for fourteen years with commodities continuing to be rationed after the war ended. For example, meat rationing continued until June 1954—ten years after D-Day).

I stepped out into the street. A man and woman were loading confectionary into a van. I walked over and asked them if I could buy a large jar of sweets from them.

"It's for a charity," I said. After a few questions they agreed to sell me one. "I'll also need a quantity of bags and the sweets must be wrapped separately so they won't stick together."

The lady said, "You'll need to visit one of our shops for this. We have three."

I climbed in their van and we drove to their nearest shop. The price agreed, I selected a suitable jar of sweets and a box of paper bags and set off home with a huge grin on my face, excited at the chance of a new venture.

I sold the sweets in the playground for one penny each or four pence for five in a bag. A teacher always patrolled the playground during morning and afternoon breaks, so lunch break was the best time—there was no adult supervision. My first day of business wasn't good, but by the second day word had got out to the other children and I did much better.

On the third day I was taken into the headmaster's office to be questioned. Unsmiling, he told me this had to stop. I was forbidden to sell in the playground.

The easy way around this was to get to school early and sell my sweets at the school gate outside the playground. Unwittingly, the headmaster had done me a favour. The children ran around inside the playground playing tag and chase, fighting, and kicking a football, but here, outside the gate, they stood together in a queue. I had their full attention.

The second day's sales were better than the first. Some boys put their money together, and I sold more bags of five sweets than single sweets.

Again, I was called to the headmaster's office and told I mustn't sell sweets at the gate either. This was my final warning.

Undeterred, I moved my sales pitch down the road to the bus station where most boys alighted on their way to school. Business was slow at first but picked up after a few days when word again got around. My profit was two hundred percent, but with all the restrictions placed up me it was not worth the time or effort. I'd already thought up another business scheme so when I'd sold all my sweets, I put this into practice.

My next idea was to run a raffle. A stall on Tooting market sold tea-sets, plates, and pans, and I could buy a four-piece tea-set consisting of plates, cups, and saucers in a nice presentation box for about five pounds. I bought one and took it home. Everyone liked the design, so I bought a book of raffle tickets and sold them door to door carrying the box with me so everyone could see the prize. At the cost of one shilling each, I needed to sell twenty to get a pound back and one hundred to get back the price of the tea-set. Alice helped, and we told our customers I would hold the raffle in two weeks. I hoped to sell two hundred tickets and double my money minus the small cost of the raffle tickets. I sold around one hundred and twenty tickets, so I'd made my money back and was in profit.

Now I needed a local professional person to do the draw in the presence of two witnesses. Doctor Magnet always visited the Community Hall on a Saturday. I remember him as being a large, jolly man. Originating from Canada, he ran a local practice where he was popular, well-liked and respected by his patients. The doctor was impressed with the tea-set and asked me to get him one. I charged him seven pounds—giving me a two-pound profit.

My next raffle was for a portable wireless. It was easier to carry around door to door, but I needed to find a different area in which to sell the tickets. The radio cost me four pounds. It was the first of its kind made in England and therefore highly sellable. Again, I needed to sell one hundred tickets to get my money back. The radio proved popular, and I sold over two hundred tickets. This gave me a seven-pound return on the raffle.

Once more, everything had to be above board, so I made sure there were plenty of witnesses to the draw and I used different people known by the local community.

I continued my raffle business, raffling a different item each time. Once I tried a set of bath towels, but they proved too heavy for me to carry around.

My father told me mushrooms were in short supply and were easy to grow. I could fill a book on the details of my mushroom investment and the complete disaster which followed.

However, what I learned from the Jewish people with whom I did business worked: buy in a box, sell in a box, or as I have practiced in my later business life: sell money. Why convert it to a product which you then have to sell to convert back into money (hopefully at a good profit). I don't want to go into the details of my present business life; sufficient to say I own a large finance company where every hour of the day people are paying me money.

My raffle business was making a profit, but I could never see it going big, and the endless knocking on doors tied me up during the evenings and at weekends.

When an opportunity came my way, I passed my contacts to two other lads and sold the business to them for twenty pounds, which they paid me over four weeks.

Chapter 20

Saturday Night Dances

I'd had the idea of running weekend dances at the local hall for a while but had been unable to do any research as my time had been taken up with the raffle business. Now I could take it forward.

The hall was closed and therefore available on Saturday nights. It had all the facilities needed to run a dance night but there couldn't be a bar as the premises held no license. My total outlay for an evening would be thirty-seven pounds: twenty pounds for the hire of the hall (this included the catering and insurance against damage), a further twenty pounds for the hire of a four-piece band (which would play from 7pm until 11pm with a thirty minute break), five pounds to have the tickets printed (including free advertising on the front), two pounds for the doorman, and the caterers would pay me back ten pounds.

I charged seven shillings and sixpence admittance (thirty-seven pence in today's money), so would need to sell one hundred and fifteen tickets either before the dance or on the door to draw even. This was bigger than I'd ever attempted. I had the money to pay for everything but was just getting over my disastrous mushroom growing venture. This would be much simpler.

I had some small leaflets printed (at the cost of four pounds for four hundred): 'A fantastic dance night. Not to be missed. Book early. Don't miss your chance to meet that special person. *Apply to booking agent'*. Underneath, I gave the office address of the hall. Alice and I handed out about half of these and left some in youth clubs. The bait was on the hook.

Giving these out door to door gave me a general idea of the public's enthusiasm for a local Saturday night dance. I also worked out the percentages: if I got fifty people in I'd have retrieved approximately half of my investment.

One week later I was called into the hall office to a good telling off. People had been calling in to reserve their ticket and there was no dance arranged. This showed me the locals were interested. I asked the lady at the office to please tell the people the dance would go ahead and to get their names and details or tell them she'd reserve them a ticket.

I booked the hall and paid ten pounds up front and asked her to book a four-piece band. I also booked the caterer whom I was told had catered for other events at the hall and left them a five-pound deposit. I booked the regular doorman and was assured he'd show up wearing a tuxedo, jacket and bow tie. I stressed the importance of the office turning no one away, of keeping the enquirers interest and taking a deposit for their ticket.

Being new to this type of venture, I'd forgotten about spot prizes. These were a feature of dances at this time. There would usually be four. Alice arranged this for me: four boxes of chocolates. With the dance arranged for three weeks hence, I delivered the rest of the leaflets door to door.

During the week the office took thirty bookings. The following week they took slightly fewer. The week before the dance a further twenty bookings were made. This totalled nearly eighty bookings, so I only needed around forty more to draw even. It seemed a lot of people wanted to meet that special person. By the day of the dance we had over one hundred tickets booked and another sixty or more paid on the door. In total over one hundred and eighty people came to the dance.

It surprised us how many men and women came on their own and after the last tune had played how many of these left together. Maybe they had met that special person. After expenses, I was left with twenty pounds, which doesn't sound much, but, as previously mentioned, this was twice the average weekly wage for an adult and people didn't have much spare cash for non-essentials such as going to dances.

I booked the hall, the four-piece band, and the door man, and negotiated a better price with the caterer. They were happy to pay me fifteen pounds, instead of the previous ten pounds.

The Hall committee only allowed me to run two dances a month. Organising and running the dances was uncomplicated. Occasionally one or two lads became a little rowdy but there were no serious incidents. Our doorman stopped anyone who had been drinking from coming in, but I thought it wise to employ two doormen at the front of the house.

To stop people passing their tickets on to friends or selling them after they had been admitted, we tore them in half and my sister kept the one half to keep account of how many people had attended and how much money we should have taken. Inevitably, a few halves went missing but we could cope with a small amount of fiddling.

I averaged twenty-five pounds per night clear profit—twice the average wage. (In 2018, this equates to one hundred and twenty pounds)

When Alice sold the necklace business to a local shop, I told her to keep the money. She was courting a local lad (she only ever had one boyfriend) and needed to save for her bottom drawer. This is what young ladies did in those days. I took this phrase literally and asked her many times about it. Just how much could she fit in that bottom drawer?

The dances became popular and soon a smartly dressed man approached me. He drove an expensive black car and ran dances at various venues around London. He wanted to know if I was interested in joining his company or if I would sell my venue to him at the price of eighty pounds—the net profit on four dances.

To be sure of making the right business decision, I asked around. After considering the variables, I agreed to sell but told him I would visit the dances occasionally to see the friends I'd made.

Chapter 21

Bike Frames and Fausto Coppi

I had some contacts who were doing well selling bicycles from
Claud Butler, a factory in Clapham.

The product was of the highest quality and the boys with
whom I was about to go into business were champion cyclists who
had contacts in most cycling clubs and further contacts with great
experience in the cycle trade. My new partners were friendly and
knowledgeable and were easy to do business with, but they didn't
have enough capital to secure maximum discounts from the
factory. This is where I came in. With my added investment we
gained purchasing power, leading to an overall profit of twenty
pounds per bike. Because I was a silent partner, they paid me
between five and six pounds of this, depending on the price of the
model.

We averaged ten sales per week, which was more than I
expected, but as one partner now had enough money to continue
without us, our three-way partnership ended after three months.
This was better for him as he didn't need to pay us a share of the
profits, and we parted as good friends.

Undeterred, I decided to set up on my own. However, I
came across a snag at the outset. The factory, Claud Butler,
refused to sell me any bikes. Their contract was with the
champion, whom they trusted, and they didn't want to ruin good
sales. I understood this and had to think of another way into the
business. It proved difficult to find out how this industry worked

and who was involved. I enquired in several bike shops, but no one would give me any information.

I was still a schoolboy and my ex partners had always kept me out of the way, so I had made no contacts. My search for contacts in this rapidly growing sport was now on. If you keep knocking at doors, one will eventually open. The secret isn't to give up.

One evening, whilst in the library looking at newspapers, I spotted an advert: *Wanted, bike mechanic with experience and contacts in the industry.* I'd never seen an advert for that type of job before. I made my way to the public phone box near Tooting Common and rang the phone number from there.

A gentleman answered the phone. He spoke quickly in an accent that sounded almost as if he were singing. I realised he was Italian, and I had to listen carefully to understand him. The address was the most important part. I wrote this down and made an appointment to go there the following Saturday. This would give me the chance to see around the premises, but, somehow, I would need to convert my enquiry to buying instead of assembly.

As planned, I travelled to Soho. The warehouse took some time to find, but if you don't try, you don't succeed. I wondered how it would look when a schoolboy arrived for an interview as a mechanic on specialist racing bikes and then switched over to speaking about sales.

I took a deep breath and walked into the shop at the front of the warehouse. Three men came in through the back door and looked at me.

The older man spoke in his melodic accent. "What do you want?"

Knowing they wouldn't take a schoolboy seriously, I answered, "My father's a retired racing man. He's asked me to see you about equipment and bikes." The men glanced at each other. "He couldn't come himself because he's busy at our assembly works. He's increasing our sales to other models in addition to Claud Butler."

"Okay…" The Italian men looked more interested in what I was saying.

"He wants details of Italian equipment."

The older man translated what I'd said to the younger two, whom I later found out were brothers. They hadn't assumed I was the mechanic due for the interview.

They spoke to each other in Italian, then the older man stepped forward. "We don't sell bikes, just equipment, which has already been assembled. Would that be of any use to your father's business?"

I asked if I could see the equipment so I could tell my father about it. The older man again relayed this to the brothers. They showed me around the warehouse. It held everything I wanted. We walked around shelf after shelf and rack after rack of bike frames, wheels, brake parts, handlebars, gears, inner tubes, and every part needed to build a racing bike.

I told the older man I'd deal in cash and my dad would send me with the money if he wanted to convert part of his business over to their equipment. I felt the excitement growing in the pit of my stomach.

The brothers spoke in their limited style of English, which I half understood. In less than an hour I'd opened a potential business trading Italian bicycle equipment. I left with a large bagful of literature and told them I'd return the following week.

I realised I didn't need to sell complete bikes, there were other ways to make headway in this business; I could sell bike frames.

I took the literature to three specialist bike shops and showed it to the shopkeepers, carefully assessing their reaction to the Italian bike frames and the possibility of assembling them with English wheels, brakes, gears, et cetera. The names on the frames were Italian so the bikes would look Italian despite the English parts. One shopkeeper asked me questions about quality, so I told him I'd lend him a bike frame—no charge—and he could build a bike and see for himself. My suggestion was met with an encouraging nod and a smile and the man gave me a list of what he required, including hand-worked lugs (a type of tubing—a 365 or similar). I had no idea what these were, but on my return to the warehouse importer, I took a crash course in bike frames and the lingo these experts in the business spoke, trying hard to understand the Italian-English mix. Hand-worked lugs were the parts that held the frames together. Some lugs were fancy, others more basic. I learned there were types you pumped up hard and smaller types for speed and there was a word for brakes, another for the different types of gears, or fixed wheel. Soon I had a working knowledge of the equipment and parts, but when the brothers talked about gear ratios, I kept quiet.

They showed me many types of frames specific to racing bikes. This is where the big money was. I arranged to spend time in the warehouse on a Saturday morning looking and learning. The two brothers spoke in their sing song accent and waved their arms about. It seemed they had a laugh with each sentence.

Up to now I'd found that because of my age, whenever I tried to conduct a business arrangement no one took me at my word and they always asked if I were being serious. This was followed by, 'how old are you?' When I showed them the money, people realised it wasn't a schoolboy joke and their attitude changed. It was most frustrating, but money always cements a deal and sometimes the beginning of a personal, friendly relationship.

The brothers selected a beautiful, deep red cycle frame with hand-worked lugs and wrapped it in thick, brown paper. I gave them twenty-five pounds. Of course, they thought I was doing business on behalf of my dad.

Before I left with the frame, they asked me to stay for lunch. They offered me wine to drink with my soft bread and cheese, but I politely passed on it. The brothers informed me that Italian boys of my age all drank red wine with their father at meal times. As we chatted, I told them of my dad's plans to sell their frames. This was met with smiles and nods and another expressive wave of their hands. They asked me to drop in every weekend as new bike frames and parts arrived every week.

They also spoke of an Italian relative who had just retired from racing. This was the man who had set up the family business. He was very famous. I didn't know of him but his coloured posters hung all around the room.

One brother said, "You should take posters to the shops you're dealing with."

The other brother added, "They would be proud to put up posters of such a famous man. He won the Tour-de-France and is a hero in Italy." It intrigued me to know whom they were talking about.

"His name is Fausto Coppi," the older man said, a gleam of pride in his eye.

I later found out Fausto Coppi was considered a 'god' in this sport. (3)

I was very lucky to find these two Italian brothers who traded only in Fausto's equipment direct from Italy. What a privilege.

I had no idea who this super-star was and how he was looked upon with renown and admiration, but I soon discovered his name opened doors in this business.

Travelling by bus and underground train, I delivered my frame to the shop. I'd been shown how to carry the frame with my head through the middle, but it was still awkward. The men in the shop went crazy for my poster of Fausto Coppi, especially when I told them he'd designed my bike frame in his factory in Italy.

One of them removed the brown paper, and the others crowded around and had to touch it because their hero had designed it.

"Would you sell the frame? How much?" one asked.

"Sorry it's not for sale," I told them.

They offered me forty pounds. I hesitated for effect then accepted the money.

The second man asked, "Could you get more of Fausto's frames... and posters? We can sell those too."

I said I could. I'd find out for sure. They wanted to know how soon I could let them know. I left their shop with a huge grin on my face.

The following Saturday I returned to Soho for another frame. I asked if I could buy some posters. They showed me several more of Fausto Coppi riding up a mountain trail on his bike in full racing attire and others showing him crossing a finishing line amidst crowds of cheering spectators. The brothers said that once I'd purchased ten frames, they would give me ten posters free of charge.

I still had no transport of my own and, therefore, no way of carrying more than one frame at a time. It was quite a journey across London, at least nine miles. I had sufficient funds so purchased three frames of different colours again wrapped in brown paper.

Mamma, the mother of the brothers, took a liking to me. Because my name was Don, she told them I had Italian blood and insisted I stop for something to eat every week. I gazed at my plate of steaming, home cooked spaghetti and meat sauce, my mouth watering. I'd seen nothing like this before. The plate was soon empty.

I needed to find a cheap method of transporting the bike frames from Soho to Tooting. Carrying them on buses and tube trains was time consuming and inefficient and wouldn't give a good impression to my suppliers or the retailers.

(3) Fausto Coppi was an all-round Italian racing cyclist. He excelled in both climbing and time trialing and was also a great sprinter. He won the Giro d'Italia five times (1940, 1947, 1949, 1952, 1953), the Tour de France twice (1949 and 1952), and the World Championship in 1953. Other notable times include winning the Giro di Lombardia five times, the Milan–San Remo three times, as well as wins at Paris–Roubaix and La Flèche Wallonne and setting the hour record (45.798 km) in 1942. Nobody ever equalled his mountain

cycling skill and his sprint finish, and many regard him as the greatest racing cyclist ever born.

In December 1959, Fausto was bitten by a mosquito whilst cycling. He ignored the bites and left them untreated. This turned to malaria which killed him. He was forty years old.

Chapter 22

Transport and Storage Problems

I noticed a boy around my age, Bob, was dropped off at school in a works van by his father every morning.

I walked over to the lad and asked him about his father's work.

Bob put his hands in his trouser pockets. "Dad doesn't own the van, but he can drive it around. He doesn't use it at weekends. It's parked up."

"You think he'd like to earn extra money when the van isn't being used?" I asked him.

The next day Bob told me his father was interested but thought it strange to be offered work by a schoolboy. "Dad says to call around our house and speak to him."

That same night, I set out to Balham where they lived. Bob's father was friendly but had a strong Irish accent which I found difficult to understand. I don't remember his name so will refer to him as Mr Irish. I explained my use for the van and told him everything would be clean and wrapped. He was amazed I had this business. He worked on Saturday's but was free on Sundays after he'd been to his Catholic Church.

I returned to the suppliers shop the following Saturday and arranged to pick up my stock on Sundays. The brothers were open for business seven days a week and lived in a large apartment at the back of the warehouse. This is where I met them. Mamma, who spoke only Italian, wouldn't let me leave until she had sorted me out some food. She told her sons to pack it in a bag to take with me. I paid for another frame and so now they owed me three frames. They also showed me a new type of saddle with Fausto Coppi written on the side. I immediately bought three for eight pounds each and told them I'd collect them the next day in the van.

I didn't have a clue how to get from Balham to Soho so couldn't direct my driver. Mr Irish said he'd carried out deliveries in the centre of London, so he'd ask as we went along. We got a little lost but eventually arrived at the warehouse where we loaded the stock and I received a kiss from Mamma, then we left and found a more direct route back to Balham and Tooting. The transport charge was seven pounds, so I gave my friend's father eight pounds, which brought a smile to his face. He told me he'd be free the following week if I needed him.

I now had three frames in my father's shed and had to transport them to the shop I was dealing with. It was closed on a Sunday, so I set off early on Monday morning planning to go to school later and tell them I was late because I'd been ill. I could only carry one frame at a time which caused a great deal of travelling back and forth, and the shop keeper said he only wanted two frames this week but might take another the following week.

Although my business had captured my imagination and was making a decent profit, I wasn't equipped to run it correctly. I couldn't keep missing school and running around with expensive bike frames. They would soon get damaged and I couldn't handle more than a few frames at a time. It was clear I had to change direction or give up.

I loved this business. The Italian brothers were gentlemen and Mamma was so kind and tender-hearted. She always gave me food and said I should take something home for my Dad.

One day she passed me a small bag saying my Dad would like this with bread. It was Italian cheese. I dropped it into my coat pocket and thought no more about it.

The tube train was crowded and when I sat down, it became uncomfortably warm. Soon, the most awful, pungent smell filled the carriage. I can't describe the offensive stink coming from my pocket. People moved away from me up to the other end of the carriage. I got stares and glares—I'm sure most thought I'd done something in my trousers. The odour was so strong it gave me a sore throat, and it grew worse by the minute.

My face flushed with embarrassment and I wanted to hide. When the train stopped at my station I hurried through the door, across the platform, and ran up the stairs leading out of the underground. All I needed was a swarm of flies to complete the mortifying scene. People scrambled away from me like I had a disease. When I got above ground, I threw the cheese in Tooting Bec Pond—it probably killed all the fish.

When I walked through my front door, my mother took one look at me, grabbed my coat, and threw it in the sink to wash it. It had stunk the house out.

When I returned to the warehouse the following week Mamma asked me how my Dad had enjoyed the cheese. I didn't want to hurt her feelings, so I lied and said he liked it. This got me into more trouble. She wrapped up another package of cheese for him. I thanked her and dropped it in my pocket. I couldn't stink out the carriage again, so this time I gave it to the first beggar I could find, which didn't take long. I was glad to get rid of it. I never saw that beggar sitting outside the tube station again. He was probably in hospital having his stomach removed or on oxygen. How can anything you eat smell that bad? I told Mamma my Dad had enough cheese. Had this continued, I'd have put all the beggars in London in hospital or risked killing fish every week. The experience still haunts me, and it put me off cheese for life.

I'd taken on too much with this bicycle frame business. The problem was locational; the Italians traded from Soho and I traded miles away in Tooting, South West London. I was too young to handle this kind of venture. I lacked transport and storage in what was, after all, a weekend adventure. It was no good anymore. If I were to continue, I needed an older partner

135

who had access to a vehicle, and this had to be arranged quickly or I'd lose my contacts. If you let people down, they soon change direction and you're no longer needed.

There weren't enough sales to warrant renting a storage warehouse or employing someone five days a week. I visited Mr Irish to see if he knew someone who might be interested and reliable.

I sat in his living room and poured out my problem to him.

He smiled. "I have a brother in Balham who's in the building trade. He has ample storage." He stood up. "We can see him now, at home, and look over his storage space."

Five minutes later we arrived outside a row of large storage sheds in a secure, lock-up area.

"These are used for plant storage," Mr Irish said, "but most of the plant is out on building sites."

"How much would you charge me to rent this area," I asked, pointing to an empty space at the back of a shed.

"There'll be no charge as long as you give my brother Sunday driving work."

I now had storage and transport; I was half-way there and only had to find transport from the storage units to the shops I was selling to—one in Wandsworth and one in Tooting.

Mr Irish told me, "I have several brothers and in-laws. I'll ask around and see what I can find out. Bob will let you know at school."

A couple of days later, Bob relayed the message that I should visit his Dad that night. When the school bell rang, I went straight to the house with Bob. Mr Irish told me he'd spoken to his cousin, Les, who lived two doors away in the same street. His cousin had his own bread van. He started work early, finished by mid-day, and had nothing to do in the afternoons. Outside these hours he could deliver for me any time I wanted. I asked how much the bread-man wanted to deliver from Balham to Tooting and Balham to Wandsworth—a twenty-minute journey. We agreed a price of eight pounds per delivery. To keep costs down, I would ensure there were at least two frames on for each delivery and that each was labelled correctly so the shops got the right frame. I would collect the money from the shops the following Saturday. I told the shopkeepers of my arrangements, but it still surprised them when a bread van delivered their goods. My profit remained the same as the shops only put in an order when they required at least two frames. My Italian friends got on well with Mr Irish and loved his accent, and their mother made him strong coffee.

I accompanied Les on the first few deliveries to make sure things were running smoothly but soon this was unnecessary as everything went according to plan.

Mr Irish and I organised the storage space at the storage shed and installed a rack on which to hang the frames to keep them off the ground. I developed a system with my weekday driver: the frames at the front of the rack had a 'W' written on the wrapping paper and went to Wandsworth, and those labelled with a 'T' were meant for delivery in Tooting. I paid him every time I was in Balham with Mr Irish.

Depending on how the bikes were selling at the two shops, there were busy weeks and others when there was no trade at all. It was time to increase my outlets. I knew of other specialist shops so visited them. Again, my age was a stumbling block. A schoolboy talking business didn't bode well with some shop owners, especially the ones who were experts in racing bikes, but once I produced the literature and posters of Fausto Coppi their attitude changed; they all wanted posters to put up in their shops. I took with me a Fausto Coppi saddle with his name on the side. This convinced some but others still weren't interested in doing business with a schoolboy.

Three more shops purchased posters and saddles. I didn't need transport for this. I could deliver these myself. There wasn't a great deal of profit in selling saddles, but it gave me the chance to work on the shopkeepers regarding their purchasing my bike frames. After a short while one of these relented and ordered frames but most shops bought ready built bikes from specialist contacts.

Another problem I came across was shops asking for credit and wanting to pay four weeks' later on an invoice. This was no good for me. I could sell them small items and get paid right away but would make no money with this.

I was looking to the future. I wanted to build up the business until I left school then run it full time. It would mean increasing my range, opening a wholesale, and learning to drive and purchasing a van.

This was all within reach, but, although I'd been living in Tooting for three years and was just short of thirteen, my thoughts and heart still lay in Bolton. I hadn't made many friends in London; I'd been too busy doing what I did best, although running a business was harder here than it had been in my old haunt.

I didn't do well at school, and some lessons, such as History, seemed a complete waste of time. If you keep looking back, you take up the time you should use for looking forward.

My class was taken on a visit to Hampton Court Castle. As we walked around the grand building, our teacher lectured us on King Henry VIII, telling us he'd had six wives and had killed most of them then died of a disease. *What kind of heritage is that? I thought. Why take us around a killer's castle?*

We stood looking up at a picture of him with a fat leg. The brass plaque beneath it said he had gout. The boys couldn't stop laughing.

I asked the teacher, "Why've we come to this place? A King had his wives killed so he could have another wife, and he started another religion and had Catholics slaughtered... and we're a Catholic school." It made no sense.

The teacher told me to report to the headmaster the next day, which I did. He gave me the cane on both hands for impertinence and put my name in the schoolbook.

School and I had never been a good match. I wasn't a Catholic but had thought I was standing up for them and then got the cane for it. Maybe there was more to Henry than we know. A group of boys talked about forming a hiking group at school. They would catch a train to Epsom Downs and spend the day walking over the countryside. Most of the boys joined up, and the teacher asked the others why they didn't want to join. He didn't ask me, so I decided to get a full report on their day out when they returned to school on Monday. It was so good that on the next day out only three turned up, so the teacher cancelled, and the group folded. I felt sorry for the teacher. He'd put a lot of effort into the group, but young lads had no interest in walking around the countryside. I couldn't wait to leave school.

Chapter 23

Mr Ponder, My Favourite teacher

I'd always viewed school as a complete waste of time and energy. It held me back from running my business and took up the biggest part of my day.

However, my outlook changed when a new teacher, Mr Ponder, was allocated our class. I really liked him. He showed an interest in each lad and made the lessons interesting. I attended all year without a day off.

If this teacher had taught me for a couple of years, I'd have passed my examination for grammar school. Mr Ponder became my hero. Had he wanted me to join a school group I would have—even high wire walking if there was such a group. I'd have been first in the queue. He had the look of Enoch Powell: the same hairstyle, moustache, and blue suit, with a tie and stiff collar and black leather shoes. This man was always smart and correct.

When introduced to us he called us by our surnames preceded by Mr. So, it was Mr Warner, Mr Price et cetera.

He went through a routine every lesson and never needed to raise his voice. Sometimes he asked the class if he could sit with the boys and a boy would take a part of the lesson. Everyone in the class tried their best for him and he got results from most of us. I owe him so much because it was he who suggested I studied mathematics—which I did in my twenties.

(A little late by some standards, I enrolled at Wandsworth Technical College and studied for my intermediate BSC. I didn't need the cap and gown that was for regular day boys.)

***

Another Bob comes to mind. He had passed his eleven plus and attended grammar school. This Bob was a lad I often spotted walking home from college carrying a large bag of homework. He was always happy and full of new things to tell you. When he saw me, he always asked what I was up to and how much money it made. I liked him very much.

Many years later I met him again. By now I'd moved away from London and was running a few businesses in my beloved Bolton. I had travelled to London with two employees and were interviewing people to take over the running of my new office premises.

As usual, I sat at the back of the room while the staff were doing the interviews. They interviewed a few promising applicants and then in walked Bob. He'd moved from Tooting to Clapham Common, was married and had excellent references and the same smile and easy-going nature. One of the staff read out his full name. This got my attention. Was he the same person? I looked up at this thirty-year-old, educated man. I never forget eyes. Once I saw his eyes I recognised the schoolboy I'd once known.

He was the man for the position, I had no doubt. I didn't get involved in the interview but instructed my two staff to call him back for a further talk. I was delighted to have him with my company, but I never introduced myself or took our old relationship any further.

Through the years I have sometimes wondered if I should have introduced myself, but that would have changed the whole structure of the interview and I had too much respect for this old school friend. After all his years of study I didn't want him knowing he would be working for me. He was such a nice man, very bright, and an asset to any company.

***

I was around thirteen years old when Mr Percy Ponder came into my life. It was a miracle: I rushed to school every morning and wanted more work from him—not history but subjects that interested me such as technical drawing and geometry. I asked him what books to read. He suggested I join the library and read about the world, geography, the British Empire, India, various other nations, and about explorers such as the people who discovered the history of Egypt and Africa.

(In later years I visited all these places and walked the length of Victoria falls and fished on the Zambele River.

Doctor Livingstone has a tomb inside the Tribal Trust Lands in Zimbabwe where white men don't set foot—at least I didn't see any when I conducted my own tour... only a few white South Africans who spoke Afrikaans, which sounds a little like Dutch. All this happened because Mr Ponder opened a Pandora's box for me.)

***

Now my bike-frame business had been set up, I was in profit by around thirty pounds a week, but I couldn't continue with the builder's warehouse and the bread van and call it a business. I realised I was too young for such a venture. I had the gift born in me to make a profit in business but my direction and the frustration of no one taking me seriously because of my age affected everything I set up.

One Saturday, Mr Irish and I visited the warehouse to take stock of the frames which were hanging up. I'd already decided to retire from the cycle business and do nothing but read books. I told Mr Irish, and he said he'd like a chance to take it over.

"Les and I are friendly with the Italian brothers," he said, "and my brother will lend me the money."

This was no problem for me. We worked out the stock value and what was called goodwill. Everything, including the contacts, would be his for three hundred and seventy pounds.

However, things didn't go as smoothly as we had hoped. The brother would only lend Mr Irish two hundred pounds, Les wanted a share of the action for one hundred pounds, and Les' wife wanted a share for putting up the remaining seventy pounds. Going back and forth trying to negotiate with each person was tiresome and time consuming, so I called them together for a meeting. Here was I, a teenage schoolboy coming down hard and talking business with three adults.

The outcome of our meeting was that the builder took over everything and he and the others would work things out amongst themselves.

I received my payment so that was fine. I certainly didn't invest it into more mushroom growing. Instead, I added some of my savings and purchased three lock-up garages which were already drawing rents. This gave me time to read in the Library.

I soon got fed up with doing nothing. Something had to happen... and it did.

Chapter 24

Finding a new Business

Some months later, I was introduced to a much older cousin who had just come out of the army. He brought me into contact with a few of his mates all of whom had business minds. One of them, Geoff, stood out from the rest. Geoff was full of business ideas, one of which involved a red, double-decker bus he'd purchased and parked up on his father's land just outside Tooting.

Geoff's skill in joinery proved invaluable in working on this project. He'd already removed all the seats and had created a comfortable living space with a kitchen at the far end of the bottom deck. The top deck was being converted into a large bedroom. This is when I came along.

Geoff wanted a partner to put money into his venture. If I invested in this, I would own a part of the bus. When completed, we would hire it out with Geoff included as the P.S.V. driver—much like a caravan on wheels.

This sounded simple to him, but I could see problems so decided against investing. Although I wasn't interested, my cousin kept asking me to get involved, so I agreed to go on the first outing with all his mates. We would leave for Brighton on the Friday night and sleep in the deluxe bus until Sunday. At around twenty years old, and having just completed their national service, the others were at a different stage in life. They had nothing in common with a thirteen-year-old.

We set off with several boxes of beer on board. The bus driver and I drank none, but the rest cracked open the bottles and soon most of the beer had been consumed.

The reason for the trip had been to promote investment into the venture. Unfortunately, the driver had brought along the wrong people. It became obvious that my cousin, his friend, and the two other young men who had come along had no money and were only interested in a boozy weekend.

Two of them asked my cousin why he had brought me. He told them I might invest in the project. This soon became a joke to them. I sat alone, away from the men as they swapped stories of their foreign exploits in the forces.

Again, they asked my cousin what I was doing in the bus. He told them, but they still didn't understand why a school boy would be there. I was of no importance to them and they ignored me. After several stops, we arrived at a farm near Brighton. The farmer had converted it into a caravan site with toilets, showers, hot and cold running water, and a small shop, and he was in the process of building a bar and a catering centre.

The lads hired a taxi and went into town. This gave me an opportunity to speak to Geoff. I learned he'd run out of money and thought this weekend would solve his problem. I said nothing about this but pointed out that although his bus had a small kitchen, it had no water and there were no washing facilities or a toilet. He couldn't rent it to anybody; it was incomplete.

Geoff stared out of the window, disappointed he'd spent so much money on the venture. He had no means of finishing the work.

I convinced him to take out a long-term rent on the site where we were staying. It had all the facilities his bus lacked and many more besides. Having done so he could rent out the bus. It was bigger than a caravan and had two floors, and the tenants would have everything they needed on site. He could also run a taxi service taking the people from the caravan park into Brighton and picking them up and bringing them back. This would bring in extra money and in winter he could drive the bus back to his father's yard to clean and refurbish it.

He was so impressed with my advice that he asked me to invest with him in the site rent. He also thought he might invest in more buses.

This project was not for me, but not wanting to upset him, I told him I would consider it.

The two brothers and their friend didn't return to the bus. My cousin met a girl and never came back either. (Some years later they got married, and he moved to Brighton.) Geoff and I now had the bus to ourselves. The next day I caught the train back to London. My weekend hadn't been a great success.

I decided not to go into business with anyone else but got involved with a retired Jewish man called Manny. He gave me lots of advice including 'The stormiest ship I ever sailed was partnership'. Very true.

I wanted to increase my ownership of the lock-up garages and put notices on the others saying I'd purchase them, but no one wanted to sell.

One day soon afterwards, I went to a book auction and purchased five hundred identical cookery books. Obviously, I couldn't carry these home, so I arranged for Les to pick them up in the bread van. The books stood me at approximately two shillings each which equates to ten for a pound. My investment was fifty pounds plus the hire of the van. Next, I visited shops that sold wool and ladies clothing saying they could sell my books for a pound each, keep half the money, and pay me when they sold them. I gave out around sixty books. More outlets were needed, and I had to find another way to market these books.

I spoke to Manny about it.

He said, "Leave it with me. I'll work out a sales gimmick. There's always a way to sell anything."

He came back to me after a week. "All newlyweds have to have this product. It will cement their marriage for life at the cost of only one pound plus one shilling for postage. Put an advert in the Exchange and Mart under the 'newlyweds' category."

I didn't know if they had such a category but tried, anyway. I told the magazine what the item was, and they said there was no problem in advertising a cookery book. I sent half a dozen for the staff as a goodwill gesture.

The advert didn't mention the books; it merely stated that this product was essential for a long, happy marriage and would ensure that the husband would never want to leave. The customer would only discover the item was a book when it arrived in the post. Over the next two weeks I sold around forty books, but the third week I only sold ten books, so I removed the advert.

I made enquiries and discovered the local colleges held cookery lessons and lectures, and the nearby schools taught cookery and domestic science. This was the key to selling my books.

I offered them the books for one pound each as a limited offer saying they could keep twenty percent of the money for buying new equipment. This was a gift from me. I left ten books at each school and college that had agreed to take them and returned the following week to see how the sales had progressed. Most outlets had sold some books, and a few had sold them all.

Between the cookery classes, shops, and general market book stalls, I sold most of my books at a pound less commission, and I sold the rest at half price to a food shop that had opened in Tooting market. The shopkeeper sold them all within two weeks and wanted more. This experience opened a new area in sales I hadn't previously considered.

I learned from the auctioneer that you could buy new paperback books from publishers. They sold off their unsold and over-printed stock. Purchasing and reselling them could be good business, depending on your outlets, but you had to buy large quantities. For much the same reasons as I'd had to give up my bicycle frame business, I was not yet equipped to take this on. I needed transport, storage, and to do the groundwork to open outlets such as book stands in each shop. (In later life, I came back to this, and it was a tremendous success.)

Even as a young boy, I looked at the service industry. Fortunes are made by insuring things and setting restrictions on the area of insurance and never being called out to service them before the insured period runs out.

When learning your trade as a business person you will deal with all types, some much smarter than you, others with their own ways of doing a deal. You have to listen to every word in a transaction and not miss a thing. Whatever your experience level, remember that you will meet that person who is sharper than you. It's your money they're after and you can fall into their trap. Fortunes can me made or lost in one deal. Never be upset if you do a bad deal. This is a part of the learning curve in your apprenticeship. When you lose money on a deal, you gain experience—something money can't buy.

Chapter 25

Service Industry

Window cleaning was one of the service industries which interested me. I watched the men climbing up and down their ladders with water and leathers and had the idea they might want to increase their rounds and earn more money. I asked a few and found this to be true.

I saw my printer and had some small leaflets printed: *'Surrey Window Cleaning Service now in your area. Clean, efficient service. First clean free. Please keep this leaflet for free clean. Thank you'*.

The people getting these leaflets through their doors had never heard of a free clean before. The window cleaners hadn't thought of using leaflets either. They weren't sales people. Ladies or gents would normally approach them in the street and ask them to clean their windows. My idea was to provide them with cleans all over their locality and a little way beyond.

I posted fifty leaflets around a neighbourhood then a while later went back to collect the leaflets and give them their free clean. I averaged five new customers from fifty leaflets then it was up to the window cleaner to keep them. Obviously, they were informed of the name of my company. The first clean of a house that had not had its windows washed for some time was the hardest for the window cleaner. Others had cleaned their own windows, but, once they had had their free clean, they realised the small cost was well worth the saving in time and effort.

I charged the window cleaners two pounds for every new clean I gained for them and they paid me after they had done their second clean. Sometimes I added ten cleans in an area.

I kept a book listing names and addresses of the cleans, the date and the name of the window cleaner, and what they had paid me. This kept the business straight. The time from the leafletting to being paid averaged about a month. Most cleaners were honest and hardworking, but I had a problem with one so didn't obtain further work for him.

After posting a block of fifty leaflets I would retire to the library to read. I told myself again 'the bait's on the hook'.

My parents only saw me in the mornings before school and I discarded my school reports without reading them. There was no chance of me going on to higher education. I enjoyed Mr Ponder's lessons—math's, geography, and biology—but had no interest in the other subjects. Surprisingly, I won the school biology prize, but I didn't turn up on presentation day.

The following day Mr Ponder took me to one side and enquired why. I told him my mum was not well so I couldn't come to school that night. This was a lie. I'd been putting leaflets through doors and afterwards had been reading in the library. I didn't like telling my favourite teacher a lie, I admired him too much. A few days afterwards I admitted lying and apologised.

He looked at me, his top lip twitching as he spoke. "One day you'll understand the way things should be. We'll say no more." I didn't understand what he meant and still don't, but he understood what I meant and that was good enough for me.

As I look back on my school days, I see I didn't fit in. I felt out-of-place sitting at a little desk with someone at the front of the class talking about things that had nothing to do with me and chalking them on the board. What good would it do me to learn or try to take an interest in such things? I only turned up each day because of Mr Ponder. For me, the rest of the lessons were a complete waste of time.

One morning, two careers officers came to the school and interviewed the boys in my class. My turn came and they asked me what I wanted to do when I left school.

"Have you thought of a trade?" one asked. "Would you like to do an apprenticeship in something?" They had a list of jobs on offer starting at two pounds a week.

The other said, "This could lead to you being a tradesman. What do you think of that? We could arrange an interview at the firms on our list."

My reply didn't fit the box. "I don't want anything to do with what you've told me. I'll soon be making forty pounds a week. I'm making twenty to thirty now." This was more than double the amount they were making. "Why would I want a trade paying two pounds a week?"

One of them wrote something on a notepad. The other was full of questions.

He sat upright and stared at me. "How do you make that kind of money? Are you making it up? What do you do? When did you start that?"

I was fed up of this and had said too much. The two people sitting looking at me had no clue about anything, so why should I tell them anymore? It was a waste of time. I stood up and left the room, without another word.

Later I was called to the headmaster's office. The two careers officers were present.

The first one looked up from his report. "Young man, you'll end up in trouble and will have no future."

The second one nodded his head. "My colleague is correct. You have no interest in anything. You'll drift from job to job always looking for work."

The headmaster took a deep breath and studied me. "Don, you're intelligent, that much is obvious, but you need to have control over your situation." He shrugged his shoulders. "And you don't have any."

The first man spoke again. "You'd be better off not telling us lies and silly stories."

On my way to school that morning I had collected twelve pounds from a window cleaner for clients I'd arranged for him. I already had a few pounds in my pocket because I was doing a deal purchasing three second hand cycles from a nearby shop on the way from school. As a result, I had around twenty pounds on me.

This meeting had made me late for my appointment and if I didn't hurry the shop would be closed. I sighed and took the money out of various pockets and asked the headmaster if I could go.

"I have some business up the road," I said. They looked at me, then the money, and then back to me, and as always, when money appears everything changes.

The 'no good, never going to do anything in his life', this 'job to job, no control person', this 'intelligent social misfit' left the room with his money. I wonder if the two inspectors changed their report. If they had seen something different in me, I'll never know. I never saw them again. Some years later, I sponsored a scheme at the school and provided all the sports equipment. Maybe this 'job to job, no good' had made good.

I was now fourteen and had been in London just over four years. My school life was nearly over. In those days you could leave school at fourteen or fifteen depending on if you wanted to go on to higher education. My education was out on the street, but I didn't want to leave Mr Ponder, my hero.

Over the last few months I had put my act together at school and was heading up the class rankings in several subjects. I'd written a few school plays which the boys acted out in front of the class. The lads I selected kept asking me to write more. They loved being in these silly little one act fantasy things.

Maybe I was maturing or taking stock of all the reading I was doing in the library—I thought it so wonderful that these places were free to a schoolboy and open until 7 pm. All the world and its knowledge was housed under one roof, and I could sit in the warm, switch off from the outside world, and read anything I chose. I saw this as my education. I could learn anything I wanted from the great masters—Edgar Allen Poe, C S Lewis, and Dickens et cetera all the way to Donald Duck.

I kept my library life separate from the rest of my life, where I was only interested in survival and making money, and attended every evening and on Saturdays, but I never took a book home. The librarians got used to seeing this little lad studying quietly, and they never asked him to pay for the privilege or to get a ticket. When it was time to leave, they kept the books he was reading to one side and put a slip under the counter.

I found my time there invigorating; it was a totally different life. What did I want with school? If someone had given me the choice, I would have sat in the library all day with my hero—the man who had directed me there in the first instance.

I still longed for my home in Bolton. Sometimes I'd sit in my favourite chair in the library and dream of my friends up north, my life there, Peter the horse, my little bedroom. Although this no longer filled me with tears, I still longed to return and find out if things had changed and what had happened to my friends and my coal brick business.

By now, I'd lost my Bolton accent and spoke like a Londoner. I'd also grown out of my rough ways and the anger which had been at the forefront of my personality when I arrived in London. I viewed life at a slower pace and didn't jump at the first sign of a transaction. In conversations, I let others do the talking and sifted out the real story before making a decision. My brain was still active, but I felt restricted when people came up with plans or ideas.

The war years had changed the people and culture of Great Britain. There were men with all manner of business deals. New products came onto the market. Plastic was taking over from steel, nylon had been invented, and the jet engine increased the speed and distance of air travel. Cars were faster and had totally changed design: the running boards were now eliminated, and the fenders, hood, and headlights were incorporated into the car's body rather than being added on. Clothing fashions had changed too, and we now had none-iron shirts. Jazz and skiffle music became popular (the latter using a combination of manufactured and homemade or improvised instruments). I, of course, was involved with all this. There was also more money about. People went out more, and, when you go out, you spend money.

The generation who had fought and survived the hardships of war, with rationing and little money to spend, had lived work-home-work-home lives. The young adults who were just coming of age weren't satisfied with living as their parents had. This new generation wanted to lead fuller lives—dancing, having fun, taking holidays at a new thing called Holiday Camps started by Billy Butlin, a man from South Africa.

Teddy Boy fashion hit the high streets. Young men walked out in wide shoes, brightly coloured socks, long coats, and jackets with velvet collars and cuffs, and they wore funny little string ties and danced to music known as bebop or pop.

I wanted to cash in on this new youth culture so had to make new contacts, and change direction from my schemes and deals and quick in and out involvement. I had money and was still only fourteen so was in a good position to push forward. I would take advantage of what was going on around me.

My life was about to change too. I would soon be leaving school, and I needed to live free of what many called family life. I decided that when I left school, I would leave home and set up on my own. I didn't tell my parents of my plans at this point as I didn't want to cause them stress. They saw little of me, anyway. Mother was busy in the house with the kitchen, bedrooms, and garden, and in planning my sister's wedding. Alice was involved with collecting items for her bottom draw—I never found it but gave my mother a helping hand with finances towards the wedding. My little dad spent most of his time at work painting or repairing paintings or painting all manner of pictures at home. He never spoke unless you spoke first but enjoyed spending time in the garden. He'd sit there for hours watching ants scurrying around carrying things here and there. He was superb at crossword puzzles and won a few prizes for this from the national press.

Dad's job paid him very little. His skill alone was worth much more than this. Although he'd been working at the same company for many years, when he retired, they only gave him one week's wage. Shortly after his retirement, the manager began calling at the house asking Dad to keep coming in to do certain jobs or make corrections for them. He always obliged and helped the company out of their tight spot but still got paid a pittance for his trouble and skill. His only advice to me was that I should continue with what I was doing as it seemed to suit me.

(Some years later, I purchased their council house for them and set up a weekly allowance, and, still later, got them help at the house.)

I decided to move back to Bolton, but first had to set things in order in Tooting. I sold the lock-up garages to a builder who was planning to build houses on the land opposite and needed more room for an access road. It was a good deal because he was chasing me. That's always a good thing in a transaction. Play the game. I wasn't interested in achieving a high price but started higher—you can always come down but never go up in a deal, so start higher.

I'd finished my involvement with the window cleaners. This had been good, but I had other things going on and I'd run out of leaflets. When I stopped, the cleaners badgered me to death asking for more cleans. It had taken them forever to pay me. They didn't appreciate a good thing until it ended. That's a human failing. It's only when the sun goes behind a cloud that you miss the sun.

Chapter 20

Auctions

Back in the library, I poured over the papers showing sales and auctions. You could buy household goods, and the government was selling over-stocked items manufactured for the war. I couldn't attend as I was at school, but I made enquiries and received detailed lists of forthcoming sales and items. I discovered you could put in a bid or offer before the auction so didn't have to attend. This is what I would do.

I sent the form back and received a number. I gave a guarantor, the manager at Lloyds Bank, Tooting Broadway and after visiting the bank and signing a form, I was ready to bid.

I bid on several items at one auction and failed on them all. In another I purchased eight hundred pairs of ex-army boots in all sizes. Some pairs came in a brown box and others were tied together by the laces, but all were made of the best quality leather and had a very strong toe caps. They stood me at a shilling per pair and I arranged for Les, my Irish bread man, to collect them three days after the sale date. Under my instructions my bank paid the bill, and the deal was done.

I'd always worn boots and still did so. I even wore a pair when I ran in the school races and came second. There was a good market for boots as every workman wore them and needed a quality pair. For a joke I offered my bank manager a pair. He always told me I was his favourite customer and would ask me what I was up to next. I set my sale price at two pounds per pair and if someone bought two pairs, they received a twenty-five percent discount. Most men of the day couldn't work this amount out, so I gave them twenty percent. I sold some of my boots to factories by leaving a pair in a box at the office or in reception. One factory in Mitcham near Tooting took half of them. Unfortunately for me, my feet were too small for men's boots.

The number of products for sale at these auctions was unending. You just needed money and transport so being in school and not having my own transport was a drawback, I had the option to give up, but you can only do this once and that is the end of your chance to go forward. Keeping to Saturday auctions was a nuisance, and I was ignored until I spoke to the auctioneer and told him I was bidding for my dad and had the money.

I worked out a scheme at one auction. I'd bid for multiple items, pay the fee, leave the items at the auction house and re-enter them at the next auction. This solved the transport problem. I'd simply buy and sell. Sometimes this worked and I sold the items, but if they didn't sell I re-entered them into the next auction. You only pay commission on the sale, so I kept my items on their premises for free and if I didn't get my price after three auctions, I withdrew the item or items and sold outside. I'd note who was bidding and try to do a deal with them... *not for me, I'd say, for my Dad.*

The time had come to leave home. I told my parents I'd now lived with them for four and a half years. Mum told me she knew I'd be all right, and I assured her I'd come around and visit and make sure she and Dad had enough money. Dad looked me up and down a couple of times and gave me a wink and that was that. I was nearly fifteen going on thirty-five and my official school leaving date was only a couple of months away. I wouldn't miss much so I didn't bother going in again. Now, I had my days to myself and as I would never, ever work for someone else it didn't bother me about getting school reports or certification. All that paper puts you in a box. You need to forget that 'follow the leader' routine.

The boys who left school when I did had no idea what they wanted to do or what they would be offered in the workplace. What use was all that education? They were walking naked into the world—*Yes, Sir... no Sir... I want a job, Sir... Anything will do, please, Sir.*

Some lads went on to higher education which meant they would get jobs with lots of stress. They were on the way to earning more money and wanting a bigger, better house with a bigger mortgage (and more stress and money.) The top of the range car had to be in the garage or parked at the front of the property... another loan, more worry. When they reached thirty years old, they would look forty and so on. Then the talk would switch to retiring. It must be good—this life of problems and stress and loans on one's back for life.

Epilogue A glorious life.

At the time of writing I am eighty-four years old and still opening new ventures in the United Kingdom and overseas. I'll not speak more about my age because age is of no importance to me. I'll retire when I die. Up to then I'll live the glorious life I have made for myself.

I have many more stories to tell—from the time at nearly fifteen when I left my family home and shortly afterwards when I moved back to Bolton, where I still live (except for when I stay in my holiday home in Spain).

Despite having received no fancy education, my life has been glorious. I might write of these adventures in another book. (I have written this book under a pseudonym, a nom de plume.)

After leaving Tooting I cut all ties with the South and returned to the North West. I never contacted any of my old partners; they were all gone and only memories, so I started again. It was a challenge, but that is what life is all about.

With war over, Bolton was a different place and there was more in which to invest. This time I was not a seven-year-old boy; I faced the challenge with money and business experience.

The name of this book comes from what I charged for a coal brick all those years ago. The picture on the front is the one I had to carry around with me as an evacuee.

Thank you for reading my story. I hope you have enjoyed the read as much as I have enjoyed writing it. My advice is to never grow mushrooms. If I write another book, I'll explain why!

Remember that if you keep looking down at your shoes that is what you will see. If you lift your head, you will see the world and for you it could be a wonderful experience. The sun always comes out from behind the clouds. It could be your turn in the sun.

And if it's your turn in the sun, take nothing for granted. The sun will go behind a cloud very quickly leaving you with many problems that could damage your drive and confidence. When I make a wrong business move, I blame no one but myself. I know it's easy to blame the people around you. I call that nudge and fudge. Sweep your disappointment under the carpet, look long and hard in the mirror, clear your mind, feel sorry for yourself if you want, but get up off the canvas and fight it out. If you can't do that don't attempt another business venture—you're not ready. Maybe you never will be, but you will know you have tried.

Sometimes I've listened to others around me voicing regret for not having done this or invested in that. I call them the 'if' people. They never had a go at anything. The way they use the word 'if' makes it the biggest word in the English language... not everyone is cut out for running their own business.

***

I thank everybody who showed an interest in my story, involving themselves in pushing me to write my scribbles down.

I hope it has been of interest to you, the reader.

- Don Warner (Scribbler)